Real Data

A Statistics Workbook
Based on Empirical Data

Zealure C. Holcomb

Pyrczak Publishing
P.O. Box 39731
Los Angeles, CA 90039

Although the author and publisher have made every effort to ensure the accuracy and completeness of information contained in this book, we assume no responsibility for errors, inaccuracies, omissions, or any inconsistency herein. Any slights of people, places, or organizations are unintentional.

Printed in the United States of America.

ISBN 1-884585-04-3

Contents

Continued

Introduction

This workbook is based on the assumption that you will find it more interesting to practice your computational skills using real data instead of the hypothetical data found in almost all introductory statistics books. Some instructors have hit on a partial solution to this problem by providing students with one or two real data sets—either ones that they have generated or ones that are provided for instructional purposes with popular statistical computer programs. These data sets are revisited each class meeting to be manipulated for a different purpose. But what about students who are not interested in the topic? For example, one popular computer program provides data on trends in beer sales. What could be more deadly than considering these data each week if you have little or no interest in them?[1]

This workbook provides 38 different real data sets that should be of interest to students of the social and behavioral sciences. In Part A, each data set is presented with instructions to compute a single statistic or a group of closely related statistics. These data sets are relatively small, making them suitable whether you are using calculators or computers. In Part B, several larger real data sets are provided for analysis by computer users.

How the Data Were Obtained

I scanned recent journals in the social and behavioral sciences looking for topics that (1) would likely be of interest to students, (2) could be easily grasped without a great deal of explanation, (3) were based on relatively small numbers of subjects, and (4) yielded results that the authors of the articles interpreted as being consistent with major theories and/or earlier empirical research on their topics. The authors of the selected articles were contacted for their raw data.

Cautions in Interpreting the Data

As you will learn in your statistics course, small samples are subject to more sampling error than large samples. Since most of the data sets in this book are small, caution should be exercised in

their interpretation. In addition, most of the samples were *not* selected at random from a defined population, so the generalizability of the data is limited. Finally, any one sample may provide a "fluke" result even if it was selected using the best sampling methods. Because of these problems, we look for trends across studies on a given topic before using the results to make important decisions.

This is not to say that the data in this book are meaningless. In fact, I tried to avoid "off-the-wall" data that are inconsistent with theory and earlier research. Nevertheless, before you cite the results you obtain from your calculations, I strongly encourage you to consult the journal articles in which the researchers originally presented the results of their analyses. There you will find discussions of other literature on the topics, the researchers' hypotheses or research purposes, and their interpretations. You will find references to these articles on the first page of each exercise.

In almost all cases, you will *not* be able to go to the journal articles to find the answers to the exercises in this book. This is true for three reasons. First, many exercises require you to calculate statistics not reported by the researchers in their articles. For example, a researcher may have reported means and standard deviations, but the exercise may require you to construct frequency distributions. Second, in many cases, you are presented with only subsets of the data—such as the data for females only—in order to keep the data sets reasonably small. Third, I sometimes handled problems such as having only partial data for some subjects in a different way than the researchers did, resulting in a slightly different data set than they analyzed.

A Note on the Statistical Guides

I assume that you will be using a comprehensive statistics textbook while using this workbook. Thus, I have provided the statistical guides as reminders of highlights that you should recall while working through the exercises. Note that a few of

---

[1]From an instructional point of view, there are benefits to analyzing a single set of data in a variety of ways. This may be done with many of the data sets in this book. The large number of data sets provided here allows instructors and students to select ones on topics of interest to them.

the exercises require you to apply computational procedures that are not universally covered in introductory textbooks. In these cases, I have provided more extensive guidelines as well as the formulas you will need.

A Note on Rounding

You should expect some slight variation in answers due to rounding. For example, if one student maintains five decimal places throughout her work and another maintains only three places, the two answers, when rounded to two decimal places, may differ slightly in the tenths or hundredths places. You should not allow such discrepancies to disturb you as long as you have calculated each answer to *at least one more decimal place* than the number of places that you round to in your final answer.

I hope you enjoy this workbook as much as I enjoyed preparing it. Your comments and reactions may be sent to me in care of the publisher, whose address is given on the title page.

Zealure C. Holcomb

Acknowledgments

I am extremely grateful to the researchers who provided data for this book. Without their assistance, this book would not be possible.

Dr. Richard Rasor of the American River College and Robert Morman of the California State University – Los Angeles reviewed the first draft of this book and provided many useful suggestions. Errors and omissions, of course, remain the responsibility of the author.

Virginia Iorio, Robert E. King, and Ralph Carroll provided editorial assistance.

Cover and graphics by Mario Sanchez.

Exercise 1 PERCENTAGES: I

What Do People Look for in Prospective Partners? A Study of Personal Ads[1]

Statistical Guide: A percentage tells us the number of cases *per one hundred* that have some characteristic. For example, if 20.0% of the students in a school are seniors, then there are 20 seniors for each 100 students.

To calculate a percentage, divide the part by the whole, multiply by 100, and add a % sign. For example, here's how to calculate the percentages of sophomores in two schools:

	Number of Sophomores (the part)	Total Number of Students (the whole)	Calculation
School A	289	1,426	289 divided by 1426 = .20266 x 100 = 20.27%
School B	145	449	145 divided by 449 = .32293 x 100 = 32.29%

Notice that there are more sophomores in School A (289) than in School B (145). However, School B has a higher percentage of sophomores (32.29%) than School A (20.27%).

Background Notes: Researchers studied the "Companions Wanted" advertisements in a major Canadian newspaper. Among other things, they tallied how many men and how many women mentioned these characteristics of prospective partners they would like to meet: (1) age (e.g., older, younger), (2) appearance (e.g., slim, cute, sexy), (3) financial status (e.g., successful, working), and (4) emotional attractiveness (e.g., warm, considerate, romantic).

Making Predictions: Before examining the data below, predict the results you will obtain. (When scientists make predictions, they are hypothesizing.) Note that your predictions are *not* right or wrong. Rather, they represent your best guess as to the outcomes you will obtain. After you perform the calculations, you will be able to determine whether the data support your predictions.

1. Do you think that a larger percentage of men or women mentioned age in describing a prospective partner?

---

[1]Data source: Nan Zhou, Department of Business and Management, City University of Hong Kong. For more information on this topic, see Zhou, N., & Abdullah, Z. (1995). Canadian match-maker ads: The more things change, the more they remain the same. *International Journal of Advertising, 14*, 334-348.

2. Do you think that a larger percentage of men or women mentioned appearance in describing a prospective partner?

3. Do you think that a larger percentage of men or women mentioned financial status in describing a prospective partner?

4. Do you think that a larger percentage of men or women mentioned emotional attractiveness in describing a prospective partner?

Data: Advertisements placed by 165 males and 235 females were analyzed, yielding the data in Table 1.

Table 1 *Number of males and females mentioning characteristics*

	Number of males mentioning characteristic in description of prospective partner	Number of females mentioning characteristic in description of prospective partner
Age	82	127
Appearance	50	48
Financial status	19	73
Emotional attractiveness	105	167

Calculations:

5. Calculate the percentages of males and females mentioning each characteristic and write them in Table 2.

Table 2 *Percentage of males and females mentioning characteristics*

	Percentage of males mentioning characteristic in description of prospective partner	Percentage of females mentioning characteristic in description of prospective partner
Age		
Appearance		
Financial status		
Emotional attractiveness		

Checking Your Predictions:

6. Based on the percentages, was your prediction in question 1 confirmed?

7. Based on the percentages, was your prediction in question 2 confirmed?

8. Based on the percentages, was your prediction in question 3 confirmed?

9. Based on the percentages, was your prediction in question 4 confirmed?

Questions for Discussion:

10. The percentages for males and the percentages for females do not sum to 100%. Speculate on the reason for this.

11. If your work is correct, the largest percentage difference is for financial status (with a much larger percentage of females mentioning it) and the smallest difference is for age (with a slightly larger percentage of females mentioning it). Do these results surprise you? Explain.

Additional Analyses Required by Your Instructor: Your instructor may require you to perform additional analyses of the data in this exercise. If so, write the names of the statistics you are to compute and your answers in the spaces below.

12. Additional statistic to be computed:

    Answer:

13. Additional statistic to be computed:

    Answer:

Exercise 2   Percentages: II

Have Americans Lost Their Compassion for the Homeless?[1]

Statistical Guide: To review percentages, see Exercise 1.

Background Notes: A national telephone poll was conducted to examine attitudes toward the homeless. Respondents were offered $10 for participating in the poll. Among other things, the pollsters asked respondents how many "homeless panhandlers" they had encountered during the past year. They speculated that if Americans were losing their compassion for the homeless, those who had more contact with them would be less compassionate. At the end of the interview, some respondents spontaneously asked the researchers to donate their $10 fee to an organization for the homeless. The pollsters used this as a measure of compassion—those who offered to donate their fee were regarded as more compassionate than those who did not offer.

Making a Prediction: Before examining the data below, predict the results you will obtain. (When scientists make predictions, they are hypothesizing.) Note that your prediction is *not* right or wrong. Rather, it represents your best guess as to the outcome you will obtain. After you perform the calculations, you will be able to determine whether the data support your prediction.

1. Predict which group had a higher percentage of respondents spontaneously offering to donate their $10 fee to the homeless. Your choices are:
   A. The group with no encounters with "homeless panhandlers" during the past year.
   B. The group with 1 or 2 encounters with "homeless panhandlers" during the past year.
   C. The group with 3 to 10 encounters with "homeless panhandlers" during the past year.
   D. The group with more than 10 encounters with "homeless panhandlers" during the past year.

---

[1]Data source: Bruce G. Link, New York City. For more information on this topic, see Link, B. G., Schwartz, S., Moore, R., Phelan, J., Struening, E., Stueve, A., & Colten, M. E. (1995). Public knowledge, attitudes, and beliefs about homeless people: Evidence for compassion fatigue? *American Journal of Community Psychology, 23,* 533-555.

Data: Table 1 shows the *numbers* of respondents who did (YES) and did not (NO) spontaneously offer to donate their fee, classified according to how much contact they had with the homeless during the past year.

Table 1 *Number of respondents donating fee compared with number of "homeless panhandlers" encountered in the past year*

Donation of fee?	"Homeless panhandlers" encountered in past year			
	None	1 or 2	3–10	>10
YES (# of cases)	103	67	48	57
NO (# of cases)	466	349	241	172
Total number	569	416	289	229

Calculations:

2. The *numbers* shown above seem to support choice A in the list of predictions. For example, 103 of those with no encounters offered to donate their fee but only 57 of those with more than 10 encounters offered. However, the group with no encounters is larger than the group with more than 10 encounters. Thus, to check out your prediction, it is necessary to compare percentages. Calculate the percentages to one decimal place each and write them in Table 2. The first column is done for you.

Table 2 *Percentage of respondents donating fee compared with number of "homeless panhandlers" encountered in the past year*

Donation of fee?	"Homeless panhandlers" encountered in the past year			
	None	1 or 2	3–10	>10
YES (% of cases)	103/569 x 100 = 18.10% = 18.1%			
NO (% of cases)	466/569 x 100 = 81.89% = 81.9%			
Total percentage	100.0%			

3. In terms of percentages, which group exhibited the greatest degree of compassion (as defined by the researchers)?
   A. The group with no encounters.
   B. The group with 1 or 2 encounters.
   C. The group with 3 to 10 encounters.
   D. The group with more than 10 encounters.

Checking Your Prediction:

4. Based on the percentages, was your prediction correct? Explain.

Questions for Discussion:

5. Are there other ways researchers might measure "compassion for the homeless" in addition to recording whether or not respondents spontaneously offered to donate their fee?

6. Even with the offer of $10 for answering the questions about the homeless, the response rate was only 65% of the 1,507 who were contacted by phone. Does this rate surprise you? Explain.

Additional Analyses Required by Your Instructor: Your instructor may require you to perform additional analyses of the data in this exercise. If so, write the names of the statistics you are to compute and your answers in the spaces below.

7. Additional statistic to be computed:

   Answer:

8. Additional statistic to be computed:

   Answer:

Exercise 3   PROPORTIONS

Assaultive Behavior of Men and Women in Intimate Relationships[1]

Statistical Guide: A *proportion* is expressed on a scale from 0.00 to 1.00. A proportion of 0.00 corresponds to 0% and a proportion of 1.00 corresponds to 100%. Thus, for example, a proportion of .25 corresponds to 25%. To calculate a proportion, divide the number of subjects who have a certain characteristic by the total number of subjects who are being considered. For instance, if 400 of the 1,000 voters in a town are registered as Democrats, the proportion who are Democrats is calculated as follows:

$$\frac{400}{1000} = .400$$

To convert a proportion to a percentage, multiply by 100 and add a % sign. Thus, .400 x 100 = 40.0%. (See Exercise 1 to review percentages.)

Clearly proportions and percentages convey the same type of information. In the popular press and mass media, percentages—not proportions—are reported. In academic journals, percentages are also favored over proportions, but proportions are sometimes reported instead of percentages.

Background Notes: College students were asked whether they were aware of the results of several large national surveys indicating that in intimate relationships (such as dating and marriage) women assault men as frequently as men assault women. Then they were asked whether they would accept the validity of the findings of these surveys. You will be analyzing the resulting data separately for men and women.

Making Predictions: Before examining the data, predict the results you will obtain. (When scientists make predictions, they are hypothesizing.) Note that your predictions are *not* right or wrong. Rather, they represent your best guess as to the outcomes you will obtain. After you perform the calculations, you will be able to determine whether the data support your predictions.

1. Do you think that a majority of the men (a proportion of .51 or more) were aware of the finding?

2. Do you think that a majority of the women were aware of the finding?

---

[1]Data source: Martin S. Fiebert, Department of Psychology, California State University–Long Beach, Long Beach, CA. For more information on this topic, consult Fiebert, M. S. (1996). College Students' Perception of Men as Victims of Women's Assaultive Behavior. *Perceptual and Motor Skills, 82,* 49-50.

3. Do you think that a larger proportion of men *or* women were aware of the finding?

4. Do you think that a majority of the men were willing to accept the validity of the finding?

5. Do you think that a majority of the women were willing to accept the validity of the finding?

Data: The data are shown in Tables 1 and 2.

Table 1 *Numbers of men and women who were aware of the finding*

Aware of the finding	Men	Women
Yes	$n = 29$	$n = 109$
No	$n = 62$	$n = 171$

Table 2 *Numbers of men and women willing to accept the validity of the finding*

Willing to accept finding	Men	Women
Yes	$n = 64$	$n = 178$
No	$n = 27$	$n = 102$

Calculations:

6. To three decimal places, what are the proportions corresponding to the numbers of cases in Table 1? Enter the values in Table 3. The first one is done for you. Note that 91 is the total number of men.

Table 3 *Proportions of men and women who were aware of the finding*

Aware of the finding?	Men	Women
Yes	29/91 = .319	
No		

7. To three decimal places, what are the proportions corresponding to the numbers of cases in Table 2? Enter the values in Table 4.

Table 4   *Proportions of men and women willing to accept
the validity of the finding*

Willing to accept finding	Men	Women
Yes		
No		

Checking Your Predictions:

8. Do the proportions confirm your prediction in question 1?

9. Do the proportions confirm your prediction in question 2?

10. Do the proportions confirm your prediction in question 3?

11. Do the proportions confirm your prediction in question 4?

12. Do the proportions confirm your prediction in question 5?

Questions for Discussion:

13. In your opinion, do the differences between the men and women seem large enough to be considered important? Explain.

14. If you were writing a research report on the data in this exercise, would you report proportions or percentages? Explain.

Additional Analyses Required by Your Instructor: Your instructor may require you to perform additional analyses of the data in this exercise. If so, write the names of the statistics you are to compute and your answers in the spaces below.

15. Additional statistic to be computed:

   Answer:

16. Additional statistic to be computed:

Answer:

Exercise 4 BAR GRAPH FOR NOMINAL DATA

Is Binge Eating Related to Dieting?[1]

Statistical Guide: A bar graph is often used to represent nominal data (i.e., data generated by naming categories, such as people naming their gender, naming their race, etc.) Here is a bar graph for the political affiliation of registered voters in one town:

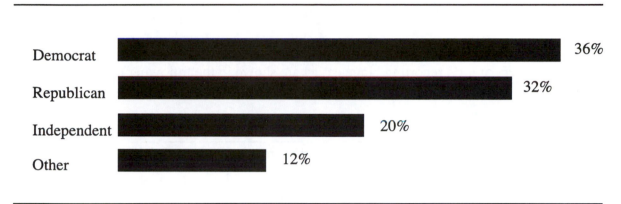

Figure 1 *Political registration in Hardship Township*

You can make a neat and accurate bar graph by using graph paper. Here's how: First, consider how wide the longest bar would be if you were to allow one space on the graph paper for each percentage. For the example shown above, the bar for the Democrats would be 36 spaces wide. You can easily manipulate this width. For example, if you want the bar to be 50% larger, multiply 36 by 1.5, which yields 54; thus, you would use 54 spaces for the Democrats. If you wanted it to be only 75% as large, multiply it by .75, which yields 27; you would make the bar for the Democrats 27 spaces wide. Of course, whatever multiplier you use with the Democrats must be used with all of the other categories.

Background Notes: Tenth-grade girls were asked whether or not they were dieting. If so, their diets were classified as either moderate (e.g., exercise, balanced diet, reduced fats), unhealthful (e.g., skipping meals, eating only one food a day), or dangerous (e.g., fasting, vomiting, using laxatives). They were also asked if they were binge eaters.

Making Predictions: Before examining the data below, predict the results you will obtain. (When scientists make predictions, they are hypothesizing.) Note that your predictions are *not* right or wrong. Rather, they represent your best guess as to the outcomes you will obtain. After

---

[1]Data source: Dianne Neumark-Sztainer, Division of General Pediatrics and Adolescent Health, The University of Minnesota, Minneapolis, MN. For more information on this topic, see Neumark-Sztainer, D., Butler, R., & Palti, H. (1995). Dieting and binge eating: Which dieters are at risk? *Journal of the American Dietetic Association, 95,* 586-589.

11

you perform the calculations, you will be able to determine whether the data support your predictions.

   1. Predict which group has the largest percentage of binge eaters.
      A. Not dieting group.
      B. Moderate diet group.
      C. Unhealthful diet group.
      D. Dangerous diet group.

   2. Predict whether the difference between the not dieting group and the dangerous diet group is large or small.

Data: The numbers of girls reporting binge eating are shown in the following table.

Table 1 *Frequencies for dieting and binge eating*

Type of diet, if any	Number reporting binge eating
No diet ($N = 158$)	24
Moderate ($N = 61$)	9
Unhealthful ($N = 95$)	23
Dangerous ($N = 27$)	12

Calculations:

   3. Calculate the percentage of girls in each group who binge eat and prepare a bar graph to illustrate the data. Plan your bar graph so that it fits in the space provided below. (You may find it easier to prepare it on a piece of graph paper and then paste it here.)

Figure 2 *Horizontal bar graph showing percentages of girls who binge eat classified according to the type of diet*

Checking Your Predictions:

4. Based on your bar graph, was your prediction in question 1 confirmed? Explain.

5. Based on your bar graph, was your prediction in question 2 confirmed? Explain.

Question for Discussion:

6. For communicating information, do you think a bar graph is more effective than just naming percentages in a paragraph? Explain.

Additional Analyses Required by Your Instructor: Your instructor may require you to perform additional analyses of the data in this exercise. If so, write the names of the statistics you are to compute and your answers in the spaces below.

7. Additional statistic to be computed:

   Answer:

8. Additional statistic to be computed:

   Answer:

Exercise 5   FREQUENCY DISTRIBUTION (UNGROUPED SCORES)

Is a Stolen Kiss a Serious Form of Sexual Harassment?[1]

Statistical Guide: A frequency distribution shows how many individuals had each score. Here's an example comparing the frequency distributions of two groups

Table 1 *Sample frequency distribution*

Score (X)	Frequency (f) for freshmen	Frequency (f) for seniors
10	55	99
9	89	105
8	105	22
7	40	17
6	10	4
	$N = 299$	$N = 247$

As you can see in Table 1, 55 freshmen and 99 seniors received a score of 10. Because there are more freshmen ($N = 299$) than seniors ($N = 247$), percentages should be calculated to facilitate the comparison of freshmen and seniors. For example, 18.4% of the freshmen had a score of 10, while 40.1% of the seniors had a score of 10. (See Exercise 1 to review percentages.) The percentages may be placed in parentheses to the right of the frequencies or may be presented in a separate table.

Background Notes: Researchers asked college students to rate the seriousness of various behaviors that may be regarded as sexually harassing when the behaviors are performed by college students. Ratings were from 1 (not serious) to 5 (very serious). One of the behaviors was "attempted or actual kissing." The researchers were interested in gender differences in perceptions regarding sexual harassment.

Making a Prediction: Before examining the data below, predict the results you will obtain. (When scientists make predictions, they are hypothesizing.) Note that your prediction is *not* right

---

[1]Data source: Diana K. Ivy, Department of Communication Arts, Texas A & M University. For more information on this topic, see Ivy, D. K., & Hamlet, S. (1996). College students and sexual dynamics: Two studies of peer sexual harassment. *Communication Education, 45,* 149-166.

or wrong. Rather, it represents your best guess as to the outcomes you will obtain. After you perform the calculations, you will be able to determine whether the data support your prediction.

1. Circle the choice that best describes your prediction regarding the seriousness that females and males attribute to attempted or actual kissing as a form of sexual harassment.
   A. Men and women are about the same.
   B. Females view it as more serious than males view it.
   C. Males view it as more serious than females view it.

Data: The scores (from 5 to 1) are given in Table 2 for the males and in Table 3 for the females.

Table 2   *Scores for males on seriousness of attempted or actual kissing*
        (5 = most serious)

5	4	5	3	5	5	5	4	2	3	5	5	5
2	4	3	5	5	5	3	4	5	5	1	4	3
5	5	4	4	4	2	3	4	2	5	3	4	5
2	5	5	2	5	4	5	2	5	5	5	4	5
2	5	5	5	5	5	3						

Table 3   *Scores for females on seriousness of attempted or actual kissing*
        (5 = most serious)

5	5	5	5	4	5	4	5	4	5	5	5	5
4	4	5	5	5	5	5	4	5	5	5	5	5
3	5	5	5	5	5	5	4	2	5	4	4	5
5	5	5	5	5	5	5	5	4	4	4	4	4
4	4	4	3	5	5	5	5	5	5	5	5	5
5	3	5	5	5	5	5	5	4	5	5	5	5
3	5	5	5	5	3	5	2	5				

Calculations:

2. Prepare a frequency distribution with separate columns for men and women. Record your work in Table 4.

Table 4 *Frequency distribution*

X	*f* for females	*f* for males

3. Convert the frequencies in Table 4 to percentages, round to one decimal place, and record them in Table 5.

Table 5 *Percentages*

X	% for females	% for males

Checking Your Prediction:

4. Based on your analysis of the data, was your prediction confirmed?

Question for Discussion:

5. Did the result surprise you? Why? Why not?

Additional Analyses Required by Your Instructor: Your instructor may require you to perform additional analyses of the data in this exercise. If so, write the names of the statistics you are to compute and your answers in the spaces on the next page.

6. Additional statistic to be computed:

Answer:

7. Additional statistic to be computed:

Answer:

Exercise 6   FREQUENCY DISTRIBUTION (GROUPED SCORES)

Basic Trust of Rape Survivors[1]

Statistical Guide: A frequency distribution organizes data to show how many individuals had each score. When the range of scores is large, we *group* the scores into *intervals*. Here are two frequency distributions with grouped scores for hypothetical samples of men and women:

Table 1 *Frequency distributions with grouped scores*

Score (X)	Frequency (f) for men	Frequency (f) for women
33-35	4	10
30-32	4	9
27-29	5	8
24-26	9	6
21-23	10	9
18-20	12	8
15-17	8	6
12-14	3	1
9-11	0	0
6-8	1	0
3-5	1	0
	N = 57	N = 57

The scores have been grouped into intervals such as 3–5, which includes scores of 3, 4, and 5. We usually group scores so that we have between 10 and 15 intervals. (In the example, there are 11 intervals.) Comparison of the frequency distributions indicates that, on the whole, women had higher scores than men.

Background Notes: Sixty-one rape survivors and 61 controls who were similar in age, education, and race were tested with the Draw-a-Person Questionnaire. All were college students. The participants were asked questions about the people they drew. Their answers were scored for a number of personality traits, including their basic trust.

Making Predictions: Before examining the data below, predict the results you will obtain. (When scientists make predictions, they are hypothesizing.) Note that your predictions are *not* right or wrong. Rather, they represent your best guess as to the outcomes you will obtain. After

[1]Data source: Stephen A. Karp, Department of Psychology, George Washington University, Washington, DC. For more information on this topic, see Karp, S. A., Silber, D. E., Holmstrom, R. W., & Stock, L. J. (1995). Personality of rape survivors as a group and by relation of survivor to perpetrator. *Journal of Clinical Psychology, 51,* 587-593.

you perform the calculations, you will be able to determine whether the data support your predictions.

1. Make a prediction about the difference you will find in basic trust between the two groups.
    A. Rape survivors will have higher basic trust scores than the controls.
    B. Rape survivors will have lower basic trust scores than the controls.
    C. Rape survivors and controls will have about the same basic trust scores.

2. If you selected choice A or B for question 1, do you think the difference will be dramatic?

Data: The basic trust scores of rape survivors and controls are given in Tables 1 and 2, respectively. Higher scores indicate higher levels of basic trust.

Table 1   *Basic trust scores of rape survivors*

43	50	42	40	37	45	30	48	28	32	42	32	47	32	42	43
32	32	50	23	40	43	35	35	20	50	35	50	30	50	32	48
47	27	33	50	42	23	40	40	40	40	42	27	35	43	40	17
35	28	47	48	33	48	38	30	45	17	43	47	42			

Table 2   *Basic trust scores of controls*

50	48	37	43	35	47	47	47	48	45	37	42	41	43	30	43
33	48	37	40	43	42	42	40	28	40	40	37	48	48	43	38
45	20	42	50	45	50	45	50	40	45	30	48	37	40	37	41
30	45	30	40	43	40	43	28	45	43	48	50	35			

Calculations:

3. Prepare a frequency distribution for the two groups. To determine the interval size, either follow the instructions in your textbook or the instructions your professor gives you. If these are not available, follow these steps:
    a. Subtract the lowest score from the highest score (e.g., if the highest score is 60 and the lowest is 24, then 60 − 24 = 36).
    b. Since we want about 15 intervals, divide the difference in the first step by 15 (e.g., 36/15 = 2.4) to estimate the interval size. Use the nearest *whole odd number* as the interval size (e.g., since 2.4 is closer to 3 than to 1, 3 is the interval size).[2]

---

[2]An odd interval size is recommended because it makes the midpoint a whole number, which makes a neater polygon, a topic treated in Exercise 8.

c. Build the intervals up from the bottom, starting with the lowest score (e.g., the bottom three-point interval is 24–26).

Place your frequency distribution in the space provided below. (You may find it easier to prepare it on a piece of lined or graph paper and paste your distribution here.) Sum the frequencies; for each group, they should sum to 61.

Table 3 *Frequency distribution of basic trust scores of rape survivors and controls*

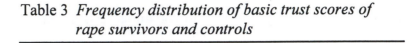

Checking Your Predictions:

4. Based on a comparison of the frequency distributions, was your prediction in question 1 confirmed? Explain.

5. Based on a comparison of the frequency distributions, was your prediction in question 2 confirmed? Explain.

Questions for Discussion:

6. Are the distributions skewed? Explain.

7. In addition to comparing frequency distributions, how else could you compare the two groups?

Additional Analyses Required by Your Instructor: Your instructor may require you to perform additional analyses of the data in this exercise. If so, write the names of the statistics you are to compute and your answers in the spaces below.

8. Additional statistic to be computed:

    Answer:

9. Additional statistic to be computed:

    Answer:

Exercise 7 CUMULATIVE FREQUENCIES, CUMULATIVE PERCENTAGES, AND PERCENTILE RANKS

Reasons People Give for Depression[1]

Statistical Guide: To review frequency distributions, see Exercise 5. We can use frequency distributions to develop percentile ranks. A percentile rank helps us compare an individual's performance with that of a group (such as a local reference group or a national norm group). For example, if a person has a percentile rank of 44, we know that he or she scored *as high as or higher than* 44 percent of those in the group. Test makers develop norms tables that often include percentile ranks. In this exercise, you will be developing percentile ranks for two depression scales by first computing cumulative frequencies and then converting them into cumulative percentages.

Background Notes: Addis, Truax, and Jacobson[1] developed a new scale measuring reasons people give for being depressed. One of the subscales is "Interpersonal Conflict." For this subscale, examinees rate each of the following six items on a 4-point scale from 1 (definitely not a reason) to 4 (definitely a reason for being depressed): "Other people don't like me," "I can't make friends," "Other people isolate me," "People treat me poorly," "People don't give me the respect I deserve," and "Other people criticize me." Another of the subscales is "Achievement," on which examinees rate these six items: "I've failed to achieve a specific goal I set for myself," "I am not fulfilling my potential," "I'm not living up to my personal standards," "I can't accomplish what I want to," "I can't get done the things I should be able to," and "I have not become the person I set out to be."

In this exercise, you will be developing percentile ranks based on the raw scores of 32 males diagnosed as having current major depression in a pilot study. (Of course, these will be preliminary percentile rank norms since a study with a much larger sample would be needed for more definitive percentile ranks for the scales.)

Making Predictions: Before examining the data below, predict the results you will obtain. (When scientists make predictions, they are hypothesizing.) Note that your predictions are *not* right or wrong. Rather, they represent your best guess as to the outcomes you will obtain. After you perform the calculations, you will be able to determine whether the data support your predictions.

1. Suppose a new client presented himself for treatment for being depressed and was administered the two subscales described above. Suppose he got a score of 10 on each scale with

---

[1]Data source: Michael E. Addis, Department of Psychology, Clark University, Worcester, MA. For more information on this topic, see Addis, M. E., Truax, P., & Jacobson, N. S. (1995). Why do people think they are depressed?: The Reasons for Depression Questionnaire. *Psychotherapy, 32,* 476-483.

possible *raw scores* ranging from 6 (all six items marked "definitely not a reason," worth 1 point each) to 24 (all six items marked "definitely a reason," worth 4 points each). Do you think he would get the same percentile rank on each subscale?
A. Yes. B. No.

2. If you answered no to question 1, do you think the percentile rank for a raw score of 10 will be higher for "Interpersonal Conflict" or higher for "Achievement"? (For example, if you answer "Interpersonal Conflict," you think that more of the 32 depressed males in the norm group had *raw scores* of 10 or less on the Interpersonal Conflict scale than on the Achievement scale.)

Data: The frequency distributions for the two subscales are shown in Table 1. The cumulative frequency (*cf*) and the cumulative percentage (*c%*) columns for the Interpersonal Conflict scale have been started for you. Note that percentile ranks are usually rounded to whole numbers.

Table 1 *Distributions on Interpersonal Conflict and Achievement*

Interpersonal Conflict				Achievement			
X	f	cf	c%	X	f	cf	c%
24	0			24	4		
23	0			23	2		
22	0			22	1		
21	1			21	5		
20	1			20	1		
19	1			19	7		
18	2			18	2		
17	1			17	1		
16	1			16	2		
15	1			15	0		
14	3			14	3		
13	3			13	2		
12	2			12	1		
11	2			11	0		
10	3	14	44%	10	1		
9	3	11	34%	9	0		
8	2	8	25%	8	0		
7	1	6	19%	7	0		
6	5	5	16%	6	0		
	N =				N =		

Calculations:

3. Complete Table 1 shown on the previous page.

4. The cumulative percentage columns show the percentile ranks. What is the percentile rank for an examinee with a raw score (*X*) of 10 on Interpersonal Conflict? (Note: Percentile ranks are *not* reported with the percentage sign. For example, if we were reporting a percentile rank to a person, we would say, "Your percentile rank is 62.")

5. What is the percentile rank for an examinee with a raw score (*X*) of 10 on Achievement?

6. What is the percentile rank for an examinee with a raw score (*X*) of 20 on Interpersonal Conflict?

7. What is the percentile rank for an examinee with a raw score (*X*) of 20 on Achievement?

Checking Your Predictions:

8. Based on your answers to questions 3 through 7, was your prediction in question 1 confirmed? Explain.

9. Based on your answers to questions 3 through 7, was your prediction in question 2 confirmed? Explain.

Questions for Discussion:

10. Do you think that someone who took the two subscales would learn more about themselves if you gave them their raw score or their percentile rank? Explain.

11. In addition to percentile ranks, have you encountered other types of scores based on norm or reference groups? If yes, name them.

Additional Analyses Required by Your Instructor: Your instructor may require you to perform additional analyses of the data in this exercise. If so, write the names of the statistics you are to compute and your answers in the spaces below.

12. Additional statistic to be computed:

Answer:

13. Additional statistic to be computed:

Answer:

Exercise 8 FREQUENCY POLYGON AND SHAPES OF DISTRIBUTIONS

Are Gamblers More Likely to Steal than Non-Gamblers?[1]

Statistical Guide: A frequency polygon is a figure drawn by connecting dots that show how many subjects had each score. In Figure 1, you can see that eight students had a score of 19, four students had a score of 20, and so on. (Note that the polygon is made to "rest" on the horizontal axis with dashed lines showing that no one scored 14 or lower and no one scored 23 or higher.)

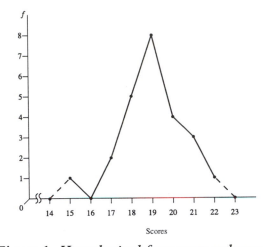

Figure 1 *Hypothetical frequency polygon*

The distribution in Figure 1 is approximately *symmetrical* with a high point in the middle. When most of the scores are concentrated at the low end with a tapering off to the right, we say the distribution is *skewed to the right* (or *has a positive skew*). When most of the scores are concentrated at the high end with a tapering off to the left, we say the distribution is *skewed to the left* (or *has a negative skew*). When drawn as a frequency polygon, a distribution is referred to as a *curve*.

When two groups of equal size are to be compared on a frequency polygon, we can draw the two curves on the same figure, using different types of lines (such as solid and dashed) or different colors of ink.[2]

Background Notes: Thirty-three 13-year-old boys were identified as gamblers because they reported gambling once a week or more, having gambled $10 or more in one day, and often or very

---

[1]Data source: Dr. Frank Vitaro, School of Psycho-Education, University of Montreal, Montreal, Canada. For more information on this topic, see Vitaro, F., Ladouceur, R., & Bujold, A. (1996). Predictive and concurrent correlates of gambling in early adolescent boys. *Journal of Early Adolescence, 16*, 211-228.
[2]When groups are unequal in size, percentages should be plotted instead of frequencies.

often gambled with nonfamily members during the previous 12 months. In this exercise, you will be comparing them to a control group of 33 13-year-old boys who were not gamblers and who were drawn at random from the same schools. All of the boys were asked a series of questions about theft on a self-report questionnaire with possible scores ranging from 10 (no theft) to 40 (much theft).

Making Predictions: Before examining the data below, predict the results you will obtain. (When scientists make predictions, they are hypothesizing.) Note that your predictions are *not* right or wrong. Rather, they represent your best guess as to the outcomes you will obtain. After you perform the calculations, you will be able to determine whether the data support your predictions.

   1. Predict which group, on the whole, reported engaging in more stealing.
      A. Gamblers. B. Non-gamblers.

   2. Predict whether the distribution for gamblers was symmetrical or skewed.

   3. If you answered "skewed" to question 2, predict whether it was skewed to the right or skewed to the left.

   4. Predict whether the distribution for non-gamblers was symmetrical or skewed.

   5. If you answered "skewed" to question 4, predict whether it was skewed to the right or skewed to the left.

Data: The frequencies (numbers of cases) are shown in Table 1 on the next page.

Table 1 *Frequency distributions of theft scores for gamblers and non-gamblers*

Theft Scores (X)	Gamblers (f)	Non-gamblers (f)
22	1	0
21	0	0
20	1	0
19	1	0
18	1	0
17	2	1
16	1	0
15	2	1
14	5	1
13	3	3
12	2	2
11	5	5
10	9	20
	n = 33	n = 33

Calculations:

6. Prepare a frequency polygon using black pencil for the gamblers and red pencil for the non-gamblers. (If you do not have colored pencils, use a dashed line for the gamblers.) Your work will be more accurate if you use graph paper and paste your answer in this space:

Checking Your Predictions:

7. Does your polygon confirm your prediction in question 1?

8. Does your polygon confirm your prediction in question 2?

9. Does your polygon confirm your prediction in question 3?

10. Does your polygon confirm your prediction in question 4?

11. Does your polygon confirm your prediction in question 5?

Question for Discussion:

12. Sometimes respondents are less than perfectly honest in their responses to self-report questionnaires. Often, they give what they perceive to be *socially desirable* answers. Suppose that in a population the distribution on theft is actually symmetrical, but the data is strongly influenced by the effects of social desirability. What type of an effect might this have on the shape of the distribution obtained by researchers?

Additional Analyses Required by Your Instructor: Your instructor may require you to perform additional analyses of the data in this exercise. If so, name the statistics you are to compute, and write your answers in the spaces below.

13. Additional statistic to be computed:

    Answer:

14. Additional statistic to be computed:

    Answer:

Exercise 9 MEAN, MEDIAN, AND SHAPES OF DISTRIBUTIONS

Average Number of Lifetime Sexual Partners of Male College Students[1]

Statistical Guide: A distribution of scores is said to be skewed to the right (i.e., positively skewed) when scores are concentrated near the low end of a distribution with a small number off to the right (toward the high end). The mean for a distribution that is skewed to the right is pulled up by the skew. A distribution of scores is said to be skewed to the left (i.e., negatively skewed) when scores are concentrated near the high end of a distribution with a small number off to the left (toward the low end). The mean for a distribution that is skewed to the left is pulled down by the skew. When a distribution is severely skewed, the mean may be an unrepresentative average. The median, in contrast, is unaffected by skewness.

Background Notes: Among other things, researchers asked a sample of college men taking an introductory psychology course how many sexual partners they have had in their lifetime. All of the men were unmarried and reported being heterosexual. Their ages ranged from 17 to 28, with a mean age of 19.

Making Predictions: Before examining the data below, predict the results you will obtain. (When scientists make predictions, they are hypothesizing.) Note that your predictions are *not* right or wrong. Rather, they represent your best guess as to the outcomes you will obtain. After you perform the calculations, you will be able to determine whether the data support your predictions.

1. Predict whether the distribution of the number of sexual partners is skewed and, if so, whether it is skewed to the right or skewed to the left.
   A. Yes, it is skewed to the right, with most men having few partners but a small number having many partners.
   B. Yes, it is skewed to the left, with most men having many partners but a small number having few partners.
   C. No, it is not skewed; it is a symmetrical distribution.

2. If your prediction to question 1 is correct, which of the following is true?
   A. The mean number of partners is higher than the median number.
   B. The median number of partners is higher than the mean number.
   C. The mean number and median number of partners are about the same.

---

[1]Data source: Dr. Sadina Rothspan, Department of Psychology, University of Southern California, Los Angeles, CA. For more information on this topic, see Rothspan, S., and Read, S. J. (1996). Present versus future time perspective and HIV risk among heterosexual college students. *Health Psychology, 15*, 131-134.

Data: Table 1 shows the frequency distribution.

Table 1 *Number of lifetime sexual partners*
for 65 male college students

Number of partners	Frequency (*f*)
88	1
25	1
21	1
20	1
15	1
12	1
11	1
10	1
7	1
6	1
5	1
4	4
3	7
2	6
1	13
0	24

Calculations:

3. What is the mean number of sexual partners? (If you are using a calculator, you can save time by multiplying each number of partners by the associated frequency and summing the products to get the sum of scores. Dividing this by 65 will yield the answer.)

4. What is the median number of sexual partners? (Ask your instructor whether he or she wants you to determine the approximate median by counting up 50% of the cases or to calculate the precise median determined with a formula that interpolates within the interval of interest.)

Checking Your Predictions:

5. Does your analysis confirm your prediction in question 1?

31

6. Does your analysis confirm your prediction in question 2?

Questions for Discussion:

7. If you were writing a report on the data in this exercise and were allowed to report only one average, would you choose the mean or the median? Explain.

8. What is the value of the mode of the distribution in this exercise? Would it be a good choice as an average for this distribution? Explain.

9. Sometimes subjects distort their replies on questionnaires to give socially desirable answers. Do you think this might have happened in this study? If so, do you think the men might have overreported or underreported the number of lifetime sexual partners they had?

Additional Analyses Required by Your Instructor: Your instructor may require you to perform additional analyses of the data in this exercise. If so, name the statistics you are to compute, and write your answers in the spaces below.

10. Additional statistic to be computed:

   Answer:

11. Additional statistic to be computed:

   Answer:

Exercise 10   MEAN AND MEDIAN

Students' Part-Time Work, GPA, and Days Absent from School[1]

Statistical Guide: The mean is the balance point in a distribution. It is a measure of "center" or "central tendency." To calculate a mean, sum the scores and divide by the number of scores.

The median also is a measure of central tendency. It is the "center score" in a distribution. To find the median, put the scores in order and count to the middle of the distribution.

Researchers usually report the mean *except* when a distribution is skewed, in which case the mean is pulled in the direction of the skew. For skewed distributions, researchers usually report the median. (To review skewed distributions, see Exercise 9).

Background Notes: In this exercise, you will be computing the mean GPA (on a scale from 0.00 to 5.00) and mean number of days absent (over a two-year period) for two groups of 12th-grade students in a high school: (1) all students who worked part-time for 10 hours or less per week and (2) all students who worked more than 20 hours per week.

Making Predictions: Before examining the data below, predict the results you will obtain. (When scientists make predictions, they are hypothesizing.) Note that your predictions are *not* right or wrong. Rather, they represent your best guess as to the outcomes you will obtain. After you perform the calculations, you will be able to determine whether the data support your predictions.

1. Do you think the average GPA for those who worked more than 20 hours per week will be *higher or lower* than the average for those who worked 10 hours or less?

2. Do you think the average number of days absent for those who worked more than 20 hours per week will be *higher or lower* than the average for those who worked 10 hour or less?

---

[1]Data source: T. F. McLaughlin, Department of Special Education, Gonzaga University, Spokane, WA. For more information on this topic, consult Lenarduzzi, G. & McLaughlin, T. F. (1996). Working on grade point average, test accuracy, and attendance of high school students. *Psychological Reports, 78*, 41-42.

Data: The data you will be analyzing are presented in Table 1.

Table 1 *GPA and days absent for two groups of students*

Worked 10 hours or less		Worked more than 20 hours	
GPA	**Days Absent**	**GPA**	**Days Absent**
4.00	88	3.33	85
1.06	110	5.00	64
2.50	77	3.67	63
2.60	27	4.50	101
5.00	66	2.80	96
4.00	45	1.33	73
4.00	34	2.67	186
4.67	74	3.00	88
1.80	41	3.60	173
2.60	18		
2.17	120		
5.00	69		
3.50	39		
2.86	116		
4.17	101		
1.80	171		
3.50	105		
4.33	96		

Calculations:

3. Calculate the means and medians of the GPAs for the two groups and enter them in Table 2. Round your answers to two decimal places.

Table 2 *Mean and median GPA*

	Worked 10 hours or less	Worked more than 20 hours
Mean		
Median		

4. Calculate the means and medians of the days absent for the two groups and enter them in Table 3. Round your answers to one decimal place.

Table 3 *Mean and median number of days absent*

	Worked 10 hours or less	Worked more than 20 hours
Mean		
Median		

Checking Your Predictions:

5. Do your answers to question 3 (Table 2) confirm your prediction in question 1? Explain.

6. Do your answers to question 4 (Table 3) confirm your prediction in question 2? Explain.

Questions for Discussion:

7. Does this study indicate that working more than 20 hours per week *causes* students to have more absences? Explain.

8. For subjects who worked more than 20 hours, the number of days absent is skewed (in particular, the students who were absent 186 and 173 days are outliers because their values are much higher than those for the bulk of the subjects). What effect does this have on the mean? Is the median affected? Which average is better for this group?

9. The number of days absent is for a two-year period. How could you calculate the *mean* number of days absent per year?

Additional Analyses Required by Your Instructor: Your instructor may require you to perform additional analyses of the data in this exercise. If so, write the names of the statistics you are to compute and your answers in the spaces below.

10. Additional statistic to be computed:

    Answer:

11. Additional statistic to be computed:

    Answer:

Exercise 11   MEAN, MEDIAN, AND MODE

Drawing Happy Faces on Restaurant Checks: Does It Increase Tips?[1]

Statistical Guide: The three averages used in statistics are the mean, the median, and the mode. Researchers usually report the mean *except* when a distribution is skewed, in which case the mean is pulled in the direction of the skew. For skewed distributions, researchers usually report the median. The mode is infrequently reported in published research.

The mean is the balance point in a distribution. It is a measure of "center" or "central tendency." To calculate a mean, sum the scores and divide by the number of scores.

The median is the "center score" in a distribution. To find it, put the scores in order and count to the middle of the distribution. (When there are ties in the middle of the distribution, this method will yield only the *approximate* median. Ask your professor whether he or she wants you to compute the approximate or *interpolated* median when there are ties.)

The mode is the most frequently occurring score. For example, if more people have a score of 10 than any other score, 10 is the mode. A distribution may have more than one mode, which is a disadvantage of this average.

Background Notes: A waitress, who worked in an upscale restaurant on a university campus at lunch time, drew a happy, smiling face on the checks of a random half of her customers. In Part A of this exercise, you will be computing the average percentage she was left as a tip under the two conditions (with a happy face and without a happy face). A waiter at the same restaurant did the same thing. In Part B of this exercise, you will be computing the average percentage he was left as a tip under the two conditions.

Making Predictions: Before examining the data below, predict the results you will obtain. (When scientists make predictions, they are hypothesizing.) Note that your predictions are *not* right or wrong. Rather, they represent your best guess as to the outcomes you will obtain. After you perform the calculations, you will be able to determine whether the data support your predictions.

1. Do you think that there was a difference in the average percentage of tips under the two conditions (happy face vs. no happy face) for the *waitress*? If yes, which condition resulted in larger tips on the average?

---

[1]Data source: Bruce Rind, Department of Psychology, Temple University. For more information on this topic, see Rind, B., & Bordia, P. (1996). Effect on restaurant tipping of male and female servers drawing a happy, smiling face on the backs of customers' checks. *Journal of Applied Social Psychology, 26,* 218-225.

2. Do you think that there was a difference in the average percentage of tips under the two conditions (happy face vs. no happy face) for the *waiter*? If yes, which condition resulted in larger tips on the average?

Data for Part A (waitress): The percentages for the waitress are shown below.

These are the tip percentages the waitress received from 23 dining parties in the *control condition* (no happy face on the check):

45%	39%	36%	34%	34%	33%	31%	31%
30%	30%	28%	28%	28%	27%	27%	25%
23%	22%	21%	21%	20%	18%	8%	

These are the tip percentages the waitress received from 22 dining parties in the *experimental condition* (happy face on the check):

72%	65%	47%	44%	41%	40%	34%	33%
33%	30%	29%	28%	27%	27%	25%	24%
24%	23%	22%	21%	21%	17%		

Calculations for Part A (waitress):

3. The mean, median, and mode for the *waitress in the control condition* are shown in the following table. Calculate the mean, median, and mode for the *experimental condition* and enter them in the appropriate cells in the table. (Keep in mind that a distribution can have more than one mode.)

Table 1   *Results for Part A (waitress)*

	Control Condition	Experimental Condition
Mean	28	
Median	28	
Mode	28	

Data for Part B (waiter): The percentages for the waiter are shown below.

These are the tip percentages the waiter received from 21 dining parties in the *control condition* (no happy face on the check):

48%	40%	38%	33%	31%	27%	23%	23%
23%	22%	21%	21%	21%	20%	18%	16%
15%	9%	0%	0%	0%			

These are the tip percentages the waiter received from 23 dining parties in the *experimental condition* (happy face on the check):

31%	27%	26%	23%	23%	21%	21%	19%
18%	18%	17%	17%	17%	16%	15%	15%
15%	14%	14%	13%	12%	9%	9%	

Calculations for Part B (waiter):

4. Calculate the means, medians, and modes for the *waiter* in the two conditions and enter them in the appropriate cells in the table. (Keep in mind that a distribution can have more than one mode.)

Table 2 *Results for Part B (waiter):*

	Control Condition	Experimental Condition
Mean		
Median		
Mode		

Checking Your Predictions for Parts A (waitress) and B (waiter):

5. Based on the *means* for the two conditions, was your prediction in question 1 (*waitress*) correct?

6. Based on the *medians* for the two conditions, was your prediction in question 1 (*waitress*) correct?

7. Based on the *means* for the two conditions, was your prediction in question 2 (*waiter*) correct?

8. Based on the *medians* for the two conditions, was your prediction in question 2 (*waiter*) correct?

Questions for Discussion:

9. If you could select only one average to describe the results of this study for the *waitress*, would you pick the mean, median, or mode? Explain your choice.

10. If you were a waiter, would you draw happy faces on the checks you give to customers? Explain.

Additional Analyses Required by Your Instructor: Your instructor may require you to perform additional analyses of the data in this exercise. If so, write the names of the statistics you are to compute and your answers in the spaces below.

11. Additional statistic to be computed:

    Answer:

12. Additional statistic to be computed:

    Answer:

Exercise 12 MEAN AND STANDARD DEVIATION FOR A POPULATION

Sudden Cardiac Deaths on the Day of a Major Earthquake[1]

Statistical Guide: The mean is the balance point in a distribution. It is the most popular average. The standard deviation is a measure of the variability of the scores around their mean. The less scores vary (that is, differ from their mean), the smaller the standard deviation. In the extreme case, if all the scores for a group are the same, then each score equals the mean and the standard deviation equals 0.00.

Background Notes: On an average day in Los Angeles, the number of sudden deaths from cardiac causes is about 4.6. On the day of the Northridge Earthquake there were 25 such deaths, 24 of which occurred after 4:31 a.m., when the earthquake struck.

Making Predictions: Before examining the data below, predict the results you will obtain. (When scientists make predictions, they are hypothesizing.) Note that your predictions are *not* right or wrong. Rather, they represent your best guess as to the outcomes you will obtain. After you perform the calculations, you will be able to determine whether the data support your predictions.

1. Predict whether the average male or the average female who died from sudden cardiac causes on the day of the earthquake was older.
   A. Average female was older. B. Average male was older.

2. Explain your reasoning for the choice you selected in question 1.

3. Predict whether the ages of the males or the ages of the females who died on the day of the earthquake were more variable.
   A. Ages of males were more variable.
   B. Ages of females were more variable.

---

[1]Data source: Robert A. Kloner, Good Samaritan Hospital, Los Angeles, CA. For more information on this topic, see Leor, J., Poole, W. K., & Kloner, R. A. (1996). Sudden cardiac death triggered by an earthquake. *The New England Journal of Medicine, 334*, 413-419. Copyright 1996 by the Massachusetts Medical Society. All rights reserved.

4. Explain your reasoning for the choice you selected in question 3.

Data: The ages of females and males who died of sudden cardiac causes after 4:31 a.m. on the day of the Northridge Earthquake are given in Tables 1 and 2, respectively.

Table 1 *Ages of females who died*

66, 92, 75, 84, 83, 80

Table 2 *Ages of males who died*

90, 38, 45, 47, 79, 75, 71, 68, 51, 55, 56, 56, 59, 67, 66, 62, 62, 64

Calculations:

5. Calculate the means and standard deviations of the ages for males and females to two decimal places and enter them in Table 3. (Note: The data are for the entire population that died after 4:31 a.m. on the day of the earthquake. Thus, you should use the formula for the standard deviation designed for use with a population and *not* the formula for estimating the population value from a sample drawn from a population.)

Table 3 *Means, standard deviations of ages of men and women who died.*

	Mean (*M*)	Standard deviation (*SD*)
Females (*N* = 6)		
Males (*N* = 18)		

6. On the average, were males or females older?

7. Were males or females more variable in their ages?

Checking Your Predictions:

8. Based on your answers, was your prediction in question 1 confirmed? Explain.

9. Based on your answers, was your prediction in question 3 confirmed? Explain.

Questions for Discussion:

10. Do the results of this study surprise you? Do you need to reconsider your reasoning in questions 2 and 4? Explain.

11. Here's a summary statement for a different study: "On the average, seniors had higher scores than freshmen, but the scores of seniors were less variable than those of the freshmen." Make a similar statement about the statistics you calculated for this exercise.

Additional Analyses Required by Your Instructor: Your instructor may require you to perform additional analyses of the data in this exercise. If so, write the names of the statistics you are to compute and your answers in the spaces below.

12. Additional statistic to be computed:

Answer:

13. Additional statistic to be computed:

Answer:

Exercise 13   MEAN AND STANDARD DEVIATION (POPULATION ESTIMATE FROM A SAMPLE)

Effects of Progressive and Sex-Object Images of Women in Advertisements[1]

Statistical Guide: See Exercise 12 to review the mean and standard deviation. In Exercise 12, you analyzed data from a population and used the basic formula for the standard deviation. When estimating the standard deviation for a population from a sample, we use a modified version of the formula (called either the *population estimate, best estimate, or unbiased estimate formula*).

Background Notes: Researchers were interested in the effects of advertisements on sex-role stereotyping. They asked a sample of college students to rate full-page color advertisements from mass circulation magazines for a variety of characteristics such as use of color, layout, etc., to maximize their attention to the ads and to distract them from the true purpose of the experiment. Some of the students rated ten sex-object ads (erotic depictions of women); some rated ten progressive ads (women being competent in non-traditional roles); others rated control ads (product-oriented with no human figures). Then all subjects took Burt's Sexual Attitude Survey, which, among other things, measures sex-role stereotyping with nine items that subjects rate on a seven-point scale from strongly agree to strongly disagree. (Sample item: "There is something wrong with a woman who does not want to marry and raise a family.") In this exercise, you will be analyzing the scores for the male subjects in the study.

Making Predictions: Before examining the data below, predict the results you will obtain. (When scientists make predictions, they are hypothesizing.) Note that your predictions are *not* right or wrong. Rather, they represent your best guess as to the outcomes you will obtain. After you perform the calculations, you will be able to determine whether the data support your predictions.

1. Predict whether the advertisements affected the sex-role stereotyping scores of the male students.
   A. Yes, it had an effect.
   B. No, it did not have an effect.

---

[1] Data source: Katherine Covell, University College of Cape Breton, Nova Scotia, Canada. For more information on this topic, see Lanis, K., & Covell, K. (1995). Images of women in advertisements: Effects on attitudes related to sexual aggression. *Sex Roles, 32*, 639-649.

2. If "yes" to question 1, predict which group had the highest mean sex-role stereotyping score.
   A. Those who rated the sex-object advertisements.
   B. Those who rated the progressive advertisements.
   C. Those who rated the control advertisements.

3. Predict which group of male students had more variability in their scores.
   A. Those who rated the sex-object advertisements.
   B. Those who rated the progressive advertisements.
   C. Those who rated the control advertisements.

Data: The scores of the males (where higher scores indicate more sex-role stereotyping) are shown in these tables:

Sex-object advertisements		Progressive advertisements		Control advertisements	
13	30	24	22	23	17
24	30	31	40	17	14
27	34	32	21	33	17
28	42	33	34	37	24
38	25	17	9	39	12
29	38	21	24	25	26
16	32	41	14	22	14
41		20		29	

Calculations:

4. Calculate the means and standard deviations to two decimal places. For the standard deviation, use the formula appropriate for estimating the population standard deviation from a sample. Enter the values in Table 1.

   You will need to calculate the sum of scores and sum of squared scores for those who viewed the sex-object advertisements in order to complete this exercise. For the convenience of those of you who are using calculators instead of computers, the sum of scores and the sum of squared scores for the other two groups are given here:

   For progressive advertisements: $\Sigma X = 383$ and $\Sigma X^2 = 10{,}995$
   For the control advertisements: $\Sigma X = 349$ and $\Sigma X^2 = 9{,}113$

Table 1 *Means and standard deviations of sex-role stereotype scores under three conditions*

	m	*s*
Sex-object advertisements ($n = 15$)		
Progressive advertisements ($n = 15$)		
Control advertisements ($n = 15$)		

Checking Your Predictions:

5. Based on the means, were your predictions in questions 1 and 2 confirmed? Explain.

6. Based on the standard deviations, was your prediction in question 3 confirmed? Explain.

Question for Discussion:

7. In your opinion, would it be worthwhile to replicate this study with larger, more demographically diverse samples? Explain.

Additional Analyses Required by Your Instructor: Your instructor may require you to perform additional analyses of the data in this exercise. If so, write the names of the statistics you are to compute and your answers in the spaces below.

8. Additional statistic to be computed:

   Answer:

9. Additional statistic to be computed:

   Answer:

Exercise 14 STANDARD SCORES

Negative Behaviors of Boys When Interacting with Their Fathers[1]

Statistical Guide: A *standard score* (also known as a *z*-score) tells us how many standard deviation units a person is from the mean of some reference group. For example, a person who has a standard score of 1.5 is one and one-half standard deviations above the mean of a group with which he or she is being compared. A person who has a standard score of -2.0 is two standard deviations below the mean of the group.

We can transform standard scores to a new scale by multiplying each standard score by a constant and then adding another constant to the product. Commonly used constants are 10 and 50. For a person with a standard score of 1.5, his or her transformed standard score is 1.5 x 10 = 15 + 50 = 65. Standard scores that are obtained by using the constants of 10 and 50 are called McCall's *T* scores.

A set of standard scores has 0.00 as its mean and 1.00 as its standard deviation. A set of transformed standard scores has the constant that you added as its mean and the constant that you multiplied by as its standard deviation.

Background Notes: Fifty-one pairs of fathers and sons were observed for 10 minutes as they discussed communication problems, spending time together, and school performance. The number of negative behaviors exhibited by each son was recorded. Examples of negative statements made by sons were "You disgust me" and "You spend too much money on stupid things."

The sons' mean age was 12.8 (SD = 0.6) and the fathers' mean age was 43.0 (SD = 4.1). All were middle-class and upper-class Caucasians.

Making a Prediction: Before examining the data below, predict the results you will obtain. (When scientists make predictions, they are hypothesizing.) Note that your prediction is *not* right or wrong. Rather, it represents your best guess as to the outcome you will obtain. After you perform the calculations, you will be able to determine whether the data support your prediction.

  1. Predict the number of negative behaviors that corresponds to a *z*-score of 0.00.
      A. 12 or more (more than about 1 per minute, on average).
      B. About 9 to 11 (about 1 per minute, on average).
      C. 8 or less (less than about 1 per minute, on average).

---

[1]Data source: Dr. Karen A. Matthews, University of Pittsburgh Medical Center, Pittsburgh, PA. For more information on this topic, see Matthews, K. A., Woodall, K. L., Kenyon, K., & Jacob, T. (1996). Negative family environment as a predictor of boys' future status on measures of hostile attitudes, interview behavior, and anger expression. *Health Psychology, 15*, 30-37.

Data: Table 1 shows the numbers of negative behaviors exhibited by the 51 boys. Before calculating the standard scores and transformed standard scores, you will need to calculate the means and standard deviations of the scores. (Use the formula for estimating the population value of the standard deviation from a sample.) To assist you in doing this, the sum of the scores and the sum of the squared scores are shown immediately below the table.

Table 1 *Raw scores (number of negative behaviors for each boy)*

9	20	9	6	19	3
23	0	8	7	9	4
1	11	13	6	13	10
5	16	15	24	8	14
2	5	14	3	27	10
7	1	5	10	19	15
4	16	13	25	0	4
17	16	3	8	2	11
12	9	1			

$\Sigma X = 512$
$\Sigma X^2 = 7,520$

Calculations:

2. To two decimal places, what is the value of the mean raw score?

3. To two decimal places, what is the value of the estimated population standard deviation?

4. To two decimal places, what is the standard score for a person with a raw score of 12?

5. Rounded to a whole number, what is the McCall's T score for a person with a raw score of 12?

6. To two decimal places, what is the standard score for a person with a raw score of 10?

7. Rounded to a whole number, what is the McCall's T score for a person with a raw score of 10?

8. To two decimal places, what is the standard score for a person with a raw score of 8?

9. Rounded to a whole number, what is the McCall's *T* score for a person with a raw score of 8?

Checking Your Prediction:

10. Does your analysis confirm your prediction in question 1?

Questions for Discussion:

11. Suppose you observed another boy interacting with his father and he obtained a standard score of +2.6. Is this high or low?

12. Suppose you observed another boy interacting with his father and he obtained a standard score of −1.99. How would you interpret his score?

Additional Analyses Required by Your Instructor: Your instructor may require you to perform additional analyses of the data in this exercise. If so, write the names of the statistics you are to compute and your answers in the spaces below.

13. Additional statistic to be computed:

    Answer:

14. Additional statistic to be computed:

    Answer:

Exercise 15   SCATTERGRAM

The Relationship Between Absences and GPA[1]

Statistical Guide: A scattergram (also known as a scatterplot or scatter diagram) is used to display the relationship between two variables. A pattern from lower-left to upper-right indicates a direct (positive) relationship. A pattern from upper-left to lower-right indicates an inverse (negative) relationship. The more scatter, the weaker the relationship, as illustrated in Figures 1 and 2.

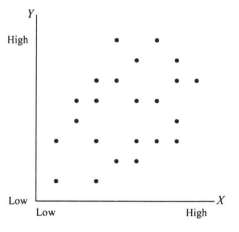

Figure 1 *A moderate to weak direct relationship*   Figure 2 *A strong inverse relationship*

Background Notes: For the 10th-grade boys in a school, these data were available: (1) GPAs on a scale from 0.0 to 5.0 and the number of days absent from school.

Making Predictions: Before examining the data below, predict the results you will obtain. (When scientists make predictions, they are hypothesizing.) Note that your predictions are *not* right or wrong. Rather, they represent your best guess as to the outcomes you will obtain. After you perform the calculations, you will be able to determine whether the data support your predictions.

1. Predict whether there is a relationship between absences and GPA.
   A. They are related. B. They are not related.

2. If you circled choice A for question 1, predict the direction of the relationship.
   A. Direct (positive) relationship. B. Inverse (negative) relationship.

3. If you circled choice A for question 1, predict how strong the relationship is.
   A. Very strong. B. Strong. C. Moderate. D. Weak. E. Very weak.

[1]Data source: T. F. McLaughlin, Department of Special Education, Gonzaga University, Spokane, WA. For more information on this topic, consult Lenarduzzi, G. & McLaughlin, T. F. (1996). Working on grade point average, test accuracy, and attendance of high school students. *Psychological Reports, 78*, 41-42.

Data: The number of absences and the GPAs are shown in the following table.

Table 1 *Absences and GPAs for 10th graders*

Student number	Days absent	GPA
1	26	1.2
2	38	1.0
3	28	4.0
4	56	1.3
5	16	3.1
6	61	3.7
7	36	1.8
8	90	3.1
9	111	1.4
10	58	2.3
11	20	4.2
12	26	4.3
13	25	2.5
14	6	3.3
15	14	2.8
16	50	2.1
17	25	4.6
18	36	3.4
19	66	3.6
20	80	2.9
21	19	4.7
22	60	1.2
23	60	1.5
24	41	2.2
25	30	1.4
26	9	4.5
27	28	2.2
28	50	3.9

Calculations:

4. Prepare a scattergram for the data. Plan your scattergram so that it fits neatly in the space provided below. (It is recommended that you draw it on graph paper and paste it in the space.) Place the absences on the horizontal axis (x axis) and the GPAs on the vertical axis (y axis). Space the number of absences and GPAs on the graph paper so that each axis is about the same length. For example, you could label the horizontal axis with absences in units of 10 such as 0, 10, 20, 30, and so on. Try allowing different numbers of spaces between 0, 10, 20, etc., until you have an appropriate length for the axis (that is, a length that will fit in the space provided and be as long as the vertical axis on which you put GPAs).

Figure 1   *Scattergram for the relationship between absences and GPAs*

Checking Your Predictions:

5. Based on your scattergram, was your prediction in question 1 confirmed? Explain.

6. Based on your scattergram, was your prediction in question 2 confirmed? Explain.

7. Based on your scattergram, was your prediction in question 3 confirmed? Explain.

Question for Discussion:

8. If your work is correct, you found that the relationship is far from perfect. Does this surprise you? Why? Why not?

Additional Analyses Required by Your Instructor: Your instructor may require you to perform additional analyses of the data in this exercise. If so, write the names of the statistics you are to compute and your answers in the spaces below.

9. Additional statistic to be computed:

   Answer:

10. Additional statistic to be computed:

    Answer:

Exercise 16 PEARSON *r*: I

Correlates of Suicide Rates[1]

Statistical Guide: The most common correlation coefficient is the Pearson *r*. When its value is positive, it indicates that those who score high on one variable tend to score high on the other. The strength of this tendency is indicated by the value of *r*. The closer it is to 1.00, the stronger the relationship; the closer it is to 0.00, the weaker it is. Correlation coefficients may also be negative. A negative value indicates that those who tend to be high on one variable tend to be low on the other. The closer the negative value is to –1.00, the stronger the relationship; the closer it is to 0.00, the weaker it is.

When the value of *r* is positive, we say that the relationship is *direct*. When it is negative, we say that it is *inverse*.

Background Notes: In this exercise, you will be correlating (1) male suicide rates with divorce rates and (2) male suicide rates with birth rates. The data are for Canadians from 1969 through 1985. The data are *rates* per some number of the population. For example, the male suicide rate in 1969 was 16 per 100,000. This means that there were, on average, 16 suicides for every 100,000 in the population.

Making Predictions: Before examining the data, predict the results you will obtain. (When scientists make predictions, they are hypothesizing.) Note that your predictions are *not* right or wrong. Rather, they represent your best guess as to the outcomes you will obtain. After you perform the calculations, you will be able to determine whether the data support your predictions.

1. Do you think that the relationship between male suicide rates and divorce rates is direct or inverse? [If you answer "direct," this means you think that (1) in years when suicide rates are higher, divorce rates are also higher, *and* (2) in years when suicide rates are lower, divorce rates are also lower. If you answer "inverse," this means you think that in years when suicide rates are higher, divorce rates are lower.]

2. Do you think that the relationship you predicted in question 1 is strong, moderate, or weak?

3. Do you think that the relationship between male suicide rates and birth rates is direct or inverse?

---

[1]Data source: David Lester, Ph.D., Center for the Study of Suicide, Blackwood, NJ. For more information on this topic, see Lester, D. (1995). Suicide rates in Canadian prisons. *Perceptual and Motor Skills*, *81*, 1230.

4. Do you think that the relationship you predicted in question 3 is strong, moderate, or weak?

Data: The data you are to analyze are presented in Table 1.

Table 1   *Canadian data on divorce rates, male suicide rates, and birth rates*

Year	Divorce rate per 10,000	Male suicide rate per 100,000	Birth rate per 1,000
1969	12	16	18
1970	14	16	18
1971	14	17	17
1972	15	17	16
1973	17	18	16
1974	20	19	16
1975	22	18	16
1976	24	18	16
1977	24	21	16
1978	24	22	15
1979	25	21	15
1980	26	21	15
1981	28	21	15
1982	29	22	15
1983	28	23	15
1984	26	21	15
1985	25	21	15

Calculations:

5. To two decimal places, what is the value of the Pearson *r* for the relationship between male suicide rates and divorce rates?

6. Does your answer to question 5 indicate a direct or inverse relationship?

7. Does your answer to question 5 indicate a strong, moderate, or weak relationship?

8. To two decimal places, what is the value of the Pearson *r* for the relationship between male suicide rates and birth rates?

9. Does your answer to question 8 indicate a direct or inverse relationship?

10. Does your answer to question 8 indicate a strong, moderate, or weak relationship?

Checking Your Predictions:

11. Do your answers to questions 5 and 6 confirm your prediction in question 1?

12. Do your answers to questions 5 and 7 confirm your prediction in question 2?

13. Do your answers to questions 8 and 9 confirm your prediction in question 3?

14. Do your answers to questions 8 and 10 confirm your prediction in question 4?

Questions for Discussion:

15. Speculate on why *rates* are reported instead of the actual numbers of divorces, suicides, and births.

16. Do the data establish that changes in divorce rates *cause* changes in suicide rates? Why? Why not?

17. Examine the data on divorce rates and birth rates, looking for trends across the years. If you were to correlate the two variables, would the Pearson *r* have a positive or negative value? Explain.

Additional Analyses Required by Your Instructor: Your instructor may require you to perform additional analyses of the data in this exercise. If so, write the names of the statistics you are to compute and your answers in the spaces below.

18. Additional statistic to be computed:

Answer:

19. Additional statistic to be computed:

Answer:

Exercise 17 PEARSON *r*: II

The Relationship Between Manic Tendencies and Eating Disorders[1]

Statistical Guide: To review the Pearson *r*, see Exercise 16.

Background Notes: Female college students were administered the American College Health Association (ACHA) eating disorders scale as well as a questionnaire that, among other things, measured manic tendencies. In this exercise you will be analyzing the ACHA scores in relation to the total scores on six true-false items on manic tendencies. Examples of the items are: "Have gone for a day with much less sleep than I normally needed and yet still not been tired" and "My mind has sometimes been so full of different ideas that I couldn't keep my attention on one topic for very long." For each statement marked true, a subject received one point. Thus, the scores could range from 0 (all items marked false) to 6 (all items marked true).

Making Predictions: Before examining the data below, predict the results you will obtain. (When scientists make predictions, they are hypothesizing.) Note that your predictions are *not* right or wrong. Rather, they represent your best guess as to the outcomes you will obtain. After you perform the calculations, you will be able to determine whether the data support your predictions.

1. Do you think the relationship between ACHA eating disorder scores and manic tendencies is direct or inverse?

2. Do you think the relationship you predicted in question 1 is strong, moderate, or weak?

---

[1]Data source: Dr. David Lester, Psychology Program, The Richard Stockton College of New Jersey, Pomona, NJ. For more information on this topic, see Williams, D., & Lester, D. (1996). Eating disorder and manic-depressive tendencies. *Psychological Reports*, *78*, 794. The data in this exercise are for only a sample of those subjects studied by Williams and Lester. For more information on the measure of manic-depressive tendencies, see Thalbourne, M. A., Delin, P.S., & Bassett, D. L. (1994). An attempt to construct scales measuring manic-depressive-like experience and behavior. *British Journal of Clinical Psychology*, *33*, 205-207. The data in this exercise are based on only selected items in the scale.

Data: Table 1 shows the scores on the ACHA eating disorders scale and the scores for each of the six items on manic tendencies. A score of 0 for an item indicates absence of the tendency because the subject marked it false; a score of 1 indicates presence of the tendency because the subject marked it true. To complete this exercise, you will need to sum the scores for the subjects in order to obtain the total manic tendencies scores; write them in the last column of Table 1.

Table 1 *Scores on the ACHA eating disorders scale and on six items that measure manic tendencies*

Subject Number	ACHA score	Scores on individual items measuring manic tendencies						Total Manic Score
		Item 1	Item 2	Item 3	Item 4	Item 5	Item 6	
1	3	0	1	1	1	1	0	
2	10	0	1	1	1	1	1	
3	9	0	1	1	0	1	0	
4	6	0	1	1	0	1	1	
5	11	1	1	1	1	1	1	
6	2	0	1	1	1	0	1	
7	3	0	1	1	1	1	1	
8	0	0	1	1	1	1	1	
9	4	0	1	1	1	1	1	
10	11	0	1	1	1	1	1	
11	8	1	1	1	1	1	1	
12	13	0	1	1	1	1	1	
13	2	0	1	1	1	1	1	
14	10	0	1	1	1	1	1	
15	8	0	1	1	1	1	1	
16	12	0	1	1	1	0	1	
17	12	1	1	1	1	1	1	
18	8	1	1	1	1	1	0	
19	11	0	1	1	0	1	1	
20	1	0	0	1	1	0	0	

Calculations:

3. To two decimal places, what is the value of the Pearson *r* for the relationship between ACHA eating disorder scores and total manic tendencies scores?

Checking Your Predictions:

4. Does your analysis confirm your prediction in question 1?

5. Does your analysis confirm your prediction in question 2?

Question for Discussion:

6. Do the results surprise you? Why? Why not?

Additional Analyses Required by Your Instructor: Your instructor may require you to perform additional analyses of the data in this exercise. If so, write the names of the statistics you are to compute and your answers in the spaces below.

7. Additional statistic to be computed:

   Answer:

8. Additional statistic to be computed:

   Answer:

Exercise 18 MULTIPLE CORRELATION

Obsessive-Compulsive Behavior and Perfectionism[1]

Statistical Guide: See Exercise 16 to review the correlation coefficient (r). While r can tell us how well one variable predicts another, a multiple correlation coefficient (R) tells us how well two or more variables in combination can predict one other variable. For all practical purposes, R is interpreted in the same way as r, keeping in mind that R is for the relationship between the combination of two or more predictors and another variable.[2]

Background Notes: The Multidimensional Perfectionism Scale was administered to 41 college men taking introductory psychology. The Maudsley Obsessive-Compulsive Inventory was also administered. Two of the traits it measures are obsessive-compulsive washing (such as repeatedly washing hands that are clean) and obsessive-compulsive checking (such as repeatedly checking something that has already been thoroughly checked).

Making Predictions: Before examining the data below, predict the results you will obtain. (When scientists make predictions, they are hypothesizing.) Note that your predictions are *not* right or wrong. Rather, they represent your best guess as to the outcomes you will obtain. After you perform the calculations, you will be able to determine whether the data support your predictions.

1. Predict the degree of relationship between obsessive-compulsive washing and perfectionism.
   A. Very strong. B. Strong. C. Moderate. D. Weak. E. Very weak.

2. Predict the degree of relationship between obsessive-compulsive checking and perfectionism.
   A. Very strong. B. Strong. C. Moderate. D. Weak. E. Very weak.

3. Predict the degree of relationship between (1) the combination of washing and checking scores and (2) perfectionism.
   A. Very strong. B. Strong. C. Moderate. D. Weak. E. Very weak.

---

[1]Data source: Dr. John Broida, Department of Psychology, University of Southern Maine, Portland, ME. For more information on this topic, see Clavin, S. L., Clavin, R. H., Gayton, W. F., & Broida, J. (1996). Continued validation of the Multidimensional Perfectionism Scale. *Psychological Reports, 78,* 732-734.

[2]The formula you will use in this exercise tells us how well the combination will work if combined in the best mathematical fashion. The mathematics of determining such a combination is beyond the scope of this book.

Data: The perfectionism, checking, and washing scores are shown in Table 1.

Table 1 *Scores on three variables for 41 college men*

Subject #	Perfectionism (Variable 1)	Washing (Variable 2)	Checking (Variable 3)	Subject #	Perfectionism (Variable 1)	Washing (Variable 2)	Checking (Variable 3)
1	100	3	5	22	100	4	0
2	130	3	6	23	114	1	5
3	90	0	3	24	103	0	1
4	116	3	5	25	123	4	2
5	94	1	3	26	106	2	0
6	96	2	4	27	98	1	2
7	103	1	0	28	123	3	7
8	107	2	5	29	112	1	1
9	110	1	6	30	115	2	1
10	82	1	0	31	111	0	1
11	116	4	6	32	105	7	2
12	134	2	4	33	110	4	5
13	111	6	4	34	118	4	4
14	74	0	2	35	106	5	7
15	95	1	4	36	95	2	6
16	85	2	0	37	107	5	4
17	107	3	1	38	94	1	0
18	111	4	1	39	86	0	0
19	105	7	5	40	89	4	0
20	96	5	3	41	88	6	1
21	85	2	1				

Calculations: For the convenience of those who are using calculators instead of computers, the sums of the scores, the sums of the squared scores, and the sums of the products of the scores are given below. Note that the subscripts indicate the variables. For example, ΣX_1 is the sum of the scores for variable 1.

$\Sigma X_1 = 4{,}250$, $\Sigma X_1^2 = 447{,}534$, $\Sigma X_2 = 109$, $\Sigma X_2^2 = 443$, $\Sigma X_3 = 117$, $\Sigma X_3^2 = 539$, $\Sigma X_1 X_2 = 11{,}553$, $\Sigma X_1 X_3 = 12{,}685$, $\Sigma X_2 X_3 = 356$

4. What is the value of the Pearson r for the relationship between variables 1 and 2? (The symbol for this is r_{12}; it indicates how well variable 2 predicts variable 1.)

5. What is the value of the Pearson r for the relationship between variables 1 and 3? (The symbol for this is r_{13}; it indicates how well variable 3 predicts variable 1.)

6. What is the value of the Pearson r for the relationship between variables 2 and 3? (The symbol for this is r_{23}; it indicates the extent of the correlation between the two predictors.)

7. What is the value of R for predicting variable 1 from the combination of variables 2 and 3? Use this formula:

$$R = \sqrt{\frac{r_{12}^2 + r_{13}^2 - 2r_{12}r_{13}r_{23}}{1 - r_{23}^2}}$$

Checking Your Predictions:

8. Do your computations confirm your prediction in question 1?

9. Do your computations confirm your prediction in question 2?

10. Do your computations confirm your prediction in question 3?

Question for Discussion:

11. Do the results surprise you? Why? Why not?

Additional Analyses Required by Your Instructor: Your instructor may require you to perform additional analyses of the data in this exercise. If so, write the names of the statistics you are to compute and your answers in the spaces below.

12. Additional statistic to be computed:

    Answer:

13. Additional statistic to be computed:

    Answer:

Exercise 19 LINEAR REGRESSION

Flexibility of Work Schedule as a Predictor of Parenting Ability[1]

Statistical Guide: When there is a relationship between two variables, we can use the scores on one of the variables to predict scores on the other. For example, college admissions officers usually have data that enable them to predict college GPAs from high school GPAs. The predictor variable is called X (in this case, high school GPA), and the criterion or outcome that is being predicted is called Y (in this case, college GPA). Using the data for those being admitted to college this year, the officer computes the intercept (a) and the slope (b) for the straight line that best describes the dots on a scattergram. (To review scattergrams, see Exercise 15). The values of a and b are then substituted in this formula:

$$Y = a + bX$$

When a new student applies, the officer predicts Y (college GPA) by substituting the student's high school GPA for X.

Background Notes: Twenty-five married women who had one or more children 18 years of age or younger and were living with a spouse or partner were subjects in a study. All of the women were employed by small banks (defined as having fewer than 100 employees), and all had occupations related to customer service (e.g., loan officer, teller, and credit card operators). Among other things, they responded to six items on *lack of flexibility in their work schedule* (sample item: "I can arrive at work and leave whenever I choose") and five items on *spillover from work to parenting* (sample item: "When I get home from work, I often do not have the energy to be a good parent"). In this exercise, you will be computing the slope and intercept of the best-fitting line that predicts spillover scores from lack of flexibility scores.

Making a Prediction: Before examining the data below, predict the results you will obtain. (When scientists make predictions, they are hypothesizing.) Note that your prediction is *not* right or wrong. Rather, it represents your best guess as to the outcome you will obtain. After you perform the calculations, you will be able to determine whether the data support your prediction.

1. Predict the type of spillover score for someone with a high score on lack of flexibility.
   A. A low spillover score. B. A moderate spillover score. C. A high spillover score.

---

[1]Data source: Dr. Shelly M. MacDermid, Department of Child Development and Family Studies, Purdue University, West Lafayette, IN. For more information on this topic, see MacDermid, S. M., Williams, M., Marks, S., & Heilbrum, G. (1994). Is small beautiful? Work-family tension, work conditions, and organizational size. *Family Relations*, *43*, 159-167.

Data: The scores are given in Table 1. Higher scores indicate greater lack of flexibility and more spillover.

Table 1 *Scores for 25 women who work in small banks*

Subject number	Lack of Flexibility score (Variable X)	Spillover from Work to Parenting score (Variable Y)
1	16	22
2	14	13
3	22	18
4	16	18
5	18	15
6	19	23
7	20	18
8	19	16
9	17	15
10	18	15
11	14	18
12	17	19
13	16	21
14	21	18
15	20	15
16	15	11
17	19	13
18	23	12
19	16	10
20	14	16
21	14	13
22	16	12
23	18	20
24	16	17
25	10	13

For the convenience of those who are using calculators instead of computers, four of the sums you will need for this exercise are given below. You will need to calculate ΣXY.
$\Sigma X = 428$, $\Sigma X^2 = 7{,}532$, $\Sigma Y = 401$, $\Sigma Y^2 = 6{,}721$

Calculations:

2. What is the value of the slope (b)?

3. What is the value of the intercept (a)?

4. For a person with a score of 20 on X (lack of flexibility), what is the *predicted* value of Y?

5. For a person with a score of 12 on X (lack of flexibility), what is the *predicted* value of Y?

Checking Your Prediction:

6. Do your computations confirm your prediction in question 1?

Question for Discussion:

7. Do the results surprise you? Why? Why not?

Additional Analyses Required by Your Instructor: Your instructor may require you to perform additional analyses of the data in this exercise. If so, write the names of the statistics you are to compute and your answers in the spaces below.

8. Additional statistic to be computed:

Answer:

9. Additional statistic to be computed:

Answer:

Exercise 20 STANDARD ERROR OF THE MEAN AND 68% CONFIDENCE INTERVAL

Effects of Instructors' Clothing on College Students' Evaluations of Instruction[1]

Statistical Guide: The standard error of the mean is a margin of error that takes account of random sampling error. For example, suppose the mean for a group is 10.00 and its standard error is 1.00. Then, we can have about 68% confidence that the true mean lies between 9.00 and 11.00. (Remember that we are not certain what the true mean is because we have sampled.) Thus, for this example, *the limits of the 68% confidence interval* are 9.00 and 11.00.

In journal articles, researchers often do not report standard errors of the means. When they report means, standard deviations, and numbers of cases, however, we can compute the associated standard errors of the means. This is done by dividing the standard deviation by the square root of the number of cases.

Background Notes: Two female and two male graduate students alternated the way they dressed while giving the same lectures to undergraduates in 12 sections of introductory psychology. The types of clothing were "formal professional" (i.e., suit and dress shoes), "casual professional" (i.e., skirt and sweater, or slacks and dark sports shirt), and "casual" (worn jeans, T-shirt, open flannel shirt, and athletic shoes). Among other things, students rated the guest lecturers on "competence" and "interesting presentation."

Making Predictions: Before examining the data below, predict the results you will obtain. (When scientists make predictions, they are hypothesizing.) Note that your predictions are *not* right or wrong. Rather, they represent your best guess as to the outcomes you will obtain. After you perform the calculations, you will be able to determine whether the data support your predictions.

1. Predict the type of clothing associated with the highest ratings on "competence."
   A. Formal professional.   B. Casual professional.   C. Casual.

2. Predict the type of clothing associated with the highest ratings on "interesting presentation."
   A. Formal professional.   B. Casual professional.   C. Casual.

---

[1]Data source: Tracy L. Morris, Department of Psychology, West Virginia University, Morgantown, WV. For more information on this topic, see Morris, T. L., Gorham, J., Cohen, S. H., & Huffman, D. (1996). Fashion in the classroom: Effects of attire on student perceptions of instructors in college classes. *Communication Education, 45,* 135-148.

Data: The data are shown in Table 1.

Table 1 *Means, standard deviations, and numbers of cases of students' ratings of guest lecturers on a 5-point scale (5 is the best score)*

	Competence	Interesting presentation
Formal professional clothing	$M = 4.29$ $s = .55$ $n = 125$	$M = 3.90$ $s = 1.08$ $n = 125$
Casual professional clothing	$M = 4.24$ $s = .60$ $n = 144$	$M = 3.93$ $s = .98$ $n = 143$
Casual clothing	$M = 4.11$ $s = .62$ $n = 132$	$M = 4.30$ $s = .89$ $n = 132$

Calculations:

3. Calculate the standard errors of the means and the limits of the 68% confidence intervals and record them in Table 2. The first two have been done for you.

Table 2 *Means, standard errors of the mean (SE_M), and 68% confidence intervals for students' ratings of guest lecturers*

	Competence	Interesting presentation
Formal professional clothing	$M = 4.29$ $SE_M = .05$ 68% C.I. = 4.24 to 4.34	$M = 3.90$ $SE_M =$ 68% C.I. =
Casual professional clothing	$M = 4.24$ $SE_M = .05$ 68% C.I. = 4.19 to 4.29	$M = 3.93$ $SE_M =$ 68% C.I. =
Casual clothing	$M = 4.11$ $SE_M =$ 68% C.I. =	$M = 4.30$ $SE_M =$ 68% C.I. =

4. You can get a *rough idea* of how reliable the differences are by comparing the confidence intervals. (Remember that a confidence interval tells us where the true mean probably lies.) For the values given to you in Table 2, you can see that the confidence intervals (4.24 to 4.34 and 4.19 to 4.29) overlap. Thus, there may not be a true difference between the two means.

Compare the confidence intervals for competence for the casual professional clothing and casual clothing conditions. Do they overlap?

5. Compare the confidence intervals for interesting presentation for the casual professional clothing and casual clothing conditions. Do they overlap?

Checking Your Predictions:

6. Based on your answers, was your prediction in question 1 confirmed? Explain.

7. Based on your answers, was your prediction in question 2 confirmed? Explain.

Question for Discussion:

8. The researchers went to great lengths to make sure that the presentations were the same in all ways except for the clothing. Is this important to know? Why? Why not?

Additional Analyses Required by Your Instructor: Your instructor may require you to perform additional analyses of the data in this exercise. If so, write the names of the statistics you are to compute and your answers in the spaces below.

9. Additional statistic to be computed:

   Answer:

10. Additional statistic to be computed:

   Answer:

Exercise 21 STANDARD ERROR OF THE MEAN AND 95% CONFIDENCE INTERVAL

Self-Acceptance and Self-Disclosure of Bisexual Men to Their Female Partners[1]

Statistical Guide: See Exercise 20 to review the standard error of the mean. In that exercise, you computed 68% confidence intervals. It is more common to use 95% confidence intervals. This means that we have 95% confidence that the true mean (without sampling error) lies within this interval. To compute a 95% confidence interval, first multiply the standard error of the mean by 1.96.[2] Then add the product to the mean to obtain the upper limit of the interval *and* subtract the product from the mean to obtain the lower limit.

Background Notes: In a sample of 280 bisexual men, 191 had not disclosed their homosexual activity to any of their female partners before having sex with them, while 89 had disclosed it to all of their female partners. Among other things, these men were asked to rate their self-acceptance of their homosexual behavior on a scale from 1 (not at all accepting) to 7 (very accepting). You will be analyzing the results to see if those who disclosed were more or less self-accepting than those who did not disclose.

Making a Prediction: Before examining the data below, predict the results you will obtain. (When scientists make predictions, they are hypothesizing.) Note that your prediction is *not* right or wrong. Rather, it represents your best guess as to the outcomes you will obtain. After you perform the calculations, you will be able to determine whether the data support your prediction.

1. Which group do you think reported having more self-acceptance of their homosexual behavior?
   A. Those who disclosed their homosexual behaviors to all their female partners before having sex with them.
   B. Those who did *not* disclose their homosexual behaviors to any of their female partners before having sex with them.

2. Explain your reasoning for the choice you selected in question 1.

---

[1]Data source: Joseph P. Stokes, Department of Psychology, University of Illinois at Chicago. For more information on this topic, see Stokes, J. P., McKirnan, D. J., Doll, L., & Burzette, R. G. (1996). Female partners of bisexual men: What they don't know might hurt them. *Psychology of Women Quarterly, 20,* 267-284.
[2]For small samples of about 60 or less, it is more precise to obtain the multiplier from a table of critical values of *t* using $df = n - 1$. Such multipliers will be somewhat greater than 1.96.

Data: The data are presented in Table 1.

Table 1 *Means, standard deviations, and number of cases for two samples of bisexual men on self-acceptance of their homosexual behavior on a scale from 1 to 7*

	Mean	Standard deviation	Number of cases
Men who disclosed to all female partners	6.46	0.97	89
Men who did not disclose to any female partners	5.14	1.73	191

Calculations:

3. Calculate the standard errors of the means and the limits of the 95% confidence intervals using a multiplier of 1.96, and record them in Table 2.

Table 2 *Standard errors of the mean and limits of the 95% confidence intervals for two samples of bisexual men*

	Standard error of the mean	Limits of the 95% confidence interval for the mean
Men who disclosed to all female partners		
Men who did not disclose to any female partners		

4. You can get a *rough idea* of how reliable the differences are by comparing the confidence intervals. (Remember that a confidence interval tells us where the true mean probably lies.) Compare the confidence intervals in your answer to question 3. Do the two confidence intervals overlap?

Checking Your Prediction:

5. Based on your answers, was your prediction in question 1 confirmed? Explain.

Questions for Discussion:

6. Do the results of this study surprise you? Do you need to reconsider your reasoning in question 2? Explain.

7. If your work is correct, you found that the 95% confidence intervals do not overlap. If you had constructed 68% confidence intervals, would they have overlapped? (You do not need to compute 68% confidence intervals to answer this question if you understand the concept of confidence intervals.)

Additional Analyses Required by Your Instructor: Your instructor may require you to perform additional analyses of the data in this exercise. If so, write the names of the statistics you are to compute and your answers in the spaces below.

8. Additional statistic to be computed:

   Answer:

9. Additional statistic to be computed:

   Answer:

Exercise 22 STANDARD ERROR OF THE MEAN AND 99% CONFIDENCE INTERVAL

Are Gay Men More Attached to Their Mothers or Their Fathers?[1]

Statistical Guide: See Exercises 20 and 21 to review the standard error of the mean. In those exercises, you computed 68% and 95% confidence intervals. It is also common to compute 99% confidence intervals. This means that we can have 99% confidence that the true mean (without sampling error) lies within this interval. To compute a 99% confidence interval, first multiply the standard error of the mean by 2.58.[2] Then add the product to the mean to obtain the upper limit of the interval, and subtract it from the mean to obtain the lower limit of the interval.

Background Notes: A sample of 72 gay young adults completed the Parental Attachment Questionnaire, which measured the quality of the parental relationships with their mothers and fathers. Higher scores indicate higher quality relationships. Nearly all the participants were White and were drawn from geographically diverse regions of the United States. The average age was in the late 20s.

Making a Prediction: Before examining the data below, predict the results you will obtain. (When scientists make predictions, they are hypothesizing.) Note that your prediction is *not* right or wrong. Rather, it represents your best guess as to the outcomes you will obtain. After you perform the calculations, you will be able to determine whether the data support your prediction.

1. Do you think that the gay men reported a higher quality relationship with their mothers or with their fathers?
   A. Mothers B. Fathers

2. Explain your reasoning for the choice you selected in question 1.

---

[1]Data source: David W. Holtzen, Department of Psychiatry, Cambridge Hospital, Harvard Medical School. For more information on this topic, see Holtzen, D. W., Kenny, M. E., & Mahalik, J. R. (1995). Contributions of parental attachment to gay or lesbian disclosure to parents and dysfunctional cognitive processes. *Journal of Counseling Psychology, 42*, 350-355.

[2]For small samples of about 60 or less, it is more precise to obtain the multiplier from a table of critical values of t using $df = n - 1$. Such multipliers will be somewhat greater than 2.58.

Data: The data are given in Table 1.

Table 1 *Means and standard deviations of scores on the Parental Attachment Questionnaire*

	Mean	Standard deviation	Number of cases
Quality of relationship with mother	186.68	31.22	72
Quality of relationship with father	177.53	40.43	72

Calculations:

3. Calculate the standard errors of the means and the limits of the 99% confidence intervals using a multiplier of 2.58, and record them in Table 2.

Table 2 *Standard errors of the means and limits of the 99% confidence intervals for the means*

	Standard error of the mean	Limits of the 99% confidence interval for the mean
Quality of relationship with mother		
Quality of relationship with father		

4. You can get a *rough idea* of how reliable the differences are by comparing the confidence intervals. (Remember that a confidence interval tells us where the true mean probably lies.) Compare the confidence intervals in your answer to question 3. Do the two confidence intervals overlap?

Checking Your Prediction:

5. Based on your answers, was your prediction in question 1 confirmed? Explain.

Questions for Discussion:

6. Do the results of this study surprise you? Do you need to reconsider your reasoning in question 2? Explain.

7. If your work is correct, you found that the 99% confidence intervals overlap. Does this mean that the 95% confidence intervals *necessarily* overlap? Explain. (You do not need to compute

95% confidence intervals to answer this question if you understand the concept of confidence intervals.)

Additional Analyses Required by Your Instructor: Your instructor may require you to perform additional analyses of the data in this exercise. If so, write the names of the statistics you are to compute and your answers in the spaces below.

8. Additional statistic to be computed:

    Answer:

9. Additional statistic to be computed:

    Answer:

Exercise 23 *t* TEST FROM DESCRIPTIVE STATISTICS FOR INDEPENDENT DATA: I

Comfort in Working with Persons with Disabilities[1]

Statistical Guide: A *t* test is used to compare two means for statistical significance. The end result of a *t* test is the probability (*p*) that the null hypothesis is correct. (The null hypothesis states that the difference between the means was created by random sampling errors.) When *p* is .05 or less, we usually reject the null hypothesis and declare the difference to be statistically significant. The *t* test for independent data (that is, two separate groups with no pairing or matching of subjects across groups) is different computationally from the *t* test for dependent data, which is considered in Exercise 26.

Background Notes: Undergraduates in management courses at two universities were surveyed to determine how comfortable they would be in working with persons with various disabilities. For each disability, students were asked to rate their level of comfort in general (*not* in terms of any specific job or work setting) on a scale from 5 (very comfortable) to 1 (very uncomfortable). Among other things, the researchers were interested in gender differences in levels of comfort. In this exercise, you will be analyzing data regarding two disabilities: epilepsy and being an amputee.

Making Predictions: Before examining the data below, predict the results you will obtain. (When scientists make predictions, they are hypothesizing.) Note that your predictions are *not* right or wrong. Rather, they represent your best guess as to the outcomes you will obtain. After you perform the calculations, you will be able to determine whether the data support your predictions.

1. Predict whether men and women differed significantly on comfort in working with persons with epilepsy.
   A. Yes, men have a significantly higher mean comfort score than women.
   B. Yes, women have a significantly higher mean comfort score than men.
   C. No, the difference between men and women is not statistically significant.

---

[1]Data source: Dr. Gwen E. Jones, Department of Management, Bowling Green State University, Bowling Green, OH. For more information on this topic, see Jones, G. E., & Stone, D. L. (1995). Perceived discomfort associated with working with persons with varying disabilities. *Perceptual and Motor Skills, 81,* 911-919.

2. Predict whether men and women differed significantly on comfort in working with persons who are amputees.

    A. Yes, men have a significantly higher mean comfort score than women.

    B. Yes, women have a significantly higher mean comfort score than men.

    C. No, the difference between men and women is not statistically significant.

Data: The descriptive statistics are shown below. Note that a higher mean indicates more comfort.

Descriptive statistics on comfort in working with persons with epilepsy:

    For 68 men: $M = 2.68, SD = 1.11$

    For 78 women: $M = 3.03, SD = 1.33$

Descriptive statistics on comfort in working with persons who are amputees:

    For 68 men: $M = 3.32, SD = 1.14$

    For 78 women: $M = 3.58, SD = 1.16$

Calculations: Your textbook may present a formula for *t* that requires you to work with the scores of individuals. The formula shown here permits you to calculate *t* using means, standard deviations, and number of cases:

$$t = \frac{M_1 - M_2}{S_{DM}}$$

Where:

$$S_{DM} = \sqrt{\left[\frac{(N_1-1)(s_1^2)+(N_2-1)(s_2^2)}{N_1+N_2-2}\right]\left[\frac{1}{N_1}+\frac{1}{N_2}\right]}$$

3. What is the observed value of *t* for the difference between the means for men and women on comfort in working with persons with epilepsy?

4. Is the difference between the means on comfort in working with persons with epilepsy statistically significant? If yes, at what probability level? (If significant, state the *highest* level; remember that .001 is higher than .01 and so on.)

5. What is the observed value of *t* for the difference between the means for men and women on comfort in working with persons who are amputees?

6. Is the difference between the means on comfort in working with persons who are amputees statistically significant? If yes, at what probability level? (If significant, state the *highest* level; remember that .001 is higher than .01 and so on.)

Checking Your Predictions:

7. Does your analysis confirm your prediction in question 1?

8. Does your analysis confirm your prediction in question 2?

Question for Discussion:

9. Do the results surprise you? Why? Why not?

Additional Analyses Required by Your Instructor: Your instructor may require you to perform additional analyses of the data in this exercise. If so, write the names of the statistics you are to compute and your answers in the spaces below.

10. Additional statistic to be computed:

   Answer:

11. Additional statistic to be computed:

   Answer:

Exercise 24 *t* TEST FROM DESCRIPTIVE STATISTICS FOR INDEPENDENT DATA: II

Hostile Feelings and Emotional Immaturity of Women with Histories of Incestuous Abuse[1]

Statistical Guide: To review the *t* test for independent data, see Exercise 23.

Background Notes: More than 700 college women were screened with a questionnaire, and 79 were identified as having a history of incestuous abuse during childhood. Another 79 women without such a history were selected as a control group. The two groups of women were administered the Apperceptive Personality Test, which yielded scores on a number of variables, among which were hostile feelings and emotional immaturity.

Making Predictions: Before examining the data below, predict the results you will obtain. (When scientists make predictions, they are hypothesizing.) Note that your predictions are *not* right or wrong. Rather, they represent your best guess as to the outcomes you will obtain. After you perform the calculations, you will be able to determine whether the data support your predictions.

1. Those who had a history of incestuous abuse had a higher mean on hostile feelings than those with no history of such abuse. Predict whether the difference is statistically significant.
   A. Yes, the difference is statistically significant at the .05 level or higher.
   B. No, the difference is not statistically significant at the .05 level.

2. Those who had a history of incestuous abuse had a higher mean on emotional immaturity than those with no history of such abuse. Predict whether the difference is statistically significant.
   A. Yes, the difference is statistically significant at the .05 level or higher.
   B. No, the difference is not statistically significant at the .05 level.

---

[1]Data source: Dr. Stephen A. Karp, Department of Psychology, The George Washington University, Washington, DC. For more information on this topic, see Karp, S. A., Holmstrom, R. W., Silber, D. E., & Stock, L. J. (1995). Personalities of women reporting incestuous abuse during childhood. *Perceptual and Motor Skills, 81,* 955-965.

Data: The descriptive statistics are shown below. Note that higher means indicate more hostile feelings and greater emotional immaturity.

Descriptive statistics on hostile feelings:

For 79 women reporting incestuous abuse: $M = 1.09$, $SD = 1.14$
For 79 control group women: $M = .75$, $SD = 1.04$

Descriptive statistics on emotional immaturity:

For 79 women reporting incestuous abuse: $M = 12.81$, $SD = 7.33$
For 79 control group women: $M = 11.07$, $SD = 7.32$

Calculations: Your textbook may present a formula for *t* that requires you to work with the scores of individuals. The formulas shown here permit you to calculate *t* using means, standard deviations, and number of cases:

$$t = \frac{M_1 - M_2}{S_{DM}}$$

Where:

$$S_{DM} = \sqrt{\left[\frac{(N_1-1)(s_1^2)+(N_2-1)(s_2^2)}{N_1+N_2-2}\right]\left[\frac{1}{N_1}+\frac{1}{N_2}\right]}$$

3. What is the observed value of *t* for the difference between the means on hostile feelings?

4. Is the difference between the means on hostile feelings statistically significant? If yes, at what probability level? (If significant, state the *highest* level; remember that .001 is higher than .01 and so on.)

5. What is the observed value of *t* for the difference between the means on emotional immaturity?

6. Is the difference between the means on emotional immaturity statistically significant? If yes, at what probability level? (If significant, state the *highest* level; remember that .001 is higher than .01 and so on.)

Checking Your Predictions:

7. Does your analysis confirm your prediction in question 1?

8. Does your analysis confirm your prediction in question 2?

Question for Discussion:

9. Do the results surprise you? Why? Why not?

Additional Analyses Required by Your Instructor: Your instructor may require you to perform additional analyses of the data in this exercise. If so, write the names of the statistics you are to compute and your answers in the spaces below.

10. Additional statistic to be computed:

Answer:

11. Additional statistic to be computed:

Answer:

Exercise 25 *t* TEST FROM RAW SCORES FOR INDEPENDENT DATA

Future Time Orientation and Condom Use for AIDS Prevention[1]

Statistical Guide: To review the *t* test for independent data, see Exercise 23.

Background Notes: Researchers administered questionnaires to college students taking an introductory psychology course. Among other things, they measured future time orientation defined as planning ahead for future events and willingness to delay gratification. (Sample item: "I believe that a person's day should be planned ahead.") They also measured condom use for AIDS prevention. (Sample item: "I am more likely to initiate the use of a condom since I've heard about AIDS.") For each variable, a higher score indicates a greater presence of the trait. In this exercise, you will be analyzing the data for some of the male subjects.

Making Predictions: Before examining the data below, predict the results you will obtain. (When scientists make predictions, they are hypothesizing.) Note that your predictions are *not* right or wrong. Rather, they represent your best guess as to the outcomes you will obtain. After you perform the calculations, you will be able to determine whether the data support your predictions.

1. Predict which group had a higher mean score on condom use for AIDS prevention.
   A. The group that had high future orientation scores.
   B. The group that had low future orientation scores.

2. Predict whether the difference you selected in question 1 is statistically significant at the .05 level or higher.
   A. Yes, the difference is statistically significant at the .05 level or higher.
   B. No, the difference is not statistically significant at the .05 level.

---

[1]Data source: Dr. Sadina Rothspan, Department of Psychology, University of Southern California, Los Angeles, CA. For more information on this topic, see Rothspan, S., and Read, S. J. (1996). Present versus future time perspective and HIV risk among heterosexual college students. *Health Psychology, 15,* 131-134.

Data: Table 1 provides the scores on rates of condom use for AIDS prevention for two groups of male subjects: (a) the eleven who had the highest scores on the future time orientation measure, with scores from 32 to 36, and (b) the ten who had the lowest scores on the future time orientation measure, with scores from 15 to 24. (Note that this is approximately 50% of the sample of men who had at least one sexual partner and for whom complete data were available. The remainder of the sample had scores from 25 to 31.)

Table 1 *Condom use scores for two groups*

Men with high future orientation scores		Men with low future orientation scores	
21	16	26	9
27	24	28	4
12	28	20	4
21	28	17	25
25	22	16	
24		23	

Calculations: To use the formulas presented in Exercises 23 and 24, you will first need to calculate the means and standard deviations. You may find that your textbook provides a formula that allows you to compute the value of *t* directly from the raw scores.

3. The mean score on condom use for AIDS prevention is higher for which group?

4. What is the observed value of *t* for the difference between the means on condom use for the two groups?

5. Is the difference between the means statistically significant? If yes, at what probability level? (If significant, state the *highest* level; remember that .001 is higher than .01 and so on.)

Checking Your Predictions:

6. Does your analysis confirm your prediction in question 1?

7. Does your analysis confirm your prediction in question 2?

Question for Discussion:

8. What are the implications, if any, of this study?

Additional Analyses Required by Your Instructor: Your instructor may require you to perform additional analyses of the data in this exercise. If so, write the names of the statistics you are to compute and your answers in the spaces below.

9. Additional statistic to be computed:

    Answer:

10. Additional statistic to be computed:

    Answer:

Exercise 26 *t* TEST FOR DEPENDENT DATA

Are Multiple-Choice Test Items
Easier than Open-Ended Items?[1]

Statistical Guide: As you know from Exercises 23 through 25, we use a *t* test to determine the statistical significance of the difference between two means. In those exercises, individuals in one group were *not* paired or matched with individuals in the other group; thus, you were conducting *t* tests for independent data. When there is pairing or matching, we conduct a *t* test for dependent (or correlated) data. For example, if we use twins in an experiment with one member of each pair of twins randomly assigned to the experimental group and the other one assigned to the control group, pairs of individuals are matched across groups. Another kind of pairing is done when we give two tests to the same individuals (such as a pretest and a posttest) and wish to test for the significance of the difference. While the computational procedures are different for an independent and a dependent *t* test, the purpose and interpretation of the two types of *t* tests are the same.[2]

Background Notes: Ten undergraduates answered the following five multiple-choice questions on a pretest at the first meeting of their statistics class, without the aid of a calculator:

> 1. What is the square of 9?
>   A. 3 B. 18 C. 81 D. 4.5 E. not given
> 2. (3.1)(0) equals
>   A. 0.0 B. 3.1 C. 3.01 D. 30.1 E. not given
> 3. 3 + 5 x 2 equals
>   A. 16 B. 30 C. 6 D. 13 E. not given
> 4. 3.5996752 rounded to the nearest hundredth is
>   A. 3.6 B. 3.59 C. 3.599 D. 3.600 E. not given
> 5. If 40 out of 60 students enjoy their statistics class, what proportion enjoys it?
>   A. 67% B. .40 C. 6.7% D. 6.6 E. not given

Then they immediately answered the same questions presented in open-ended form (without choices). Another ten undergraduates first answered the questions in the open-ended form and then in the multiple-choice form.

Making Predictions: Before examining the data below, predict the results you will obtain. (When scientists make predictions, they are hypothesizing.) Note that your predictions are *not* right or wrong. Rather, they represent your best guess as to the outcome you will obtain. After

---

[1]Data source: Dr. Fred Pyrczak, Division of Educational Foundations and Interdivisional Studies, California State University, Los Angeles, CA.

[2]To the extent that the matching is related to the variable we are measuring, a *t* test for dependent data is more likely to be significant than a *t* test for independent data because the matching reduces the potential sampling error that may explain the difference between groups.

you perform the calculations, you will be able to determine whether the data support your predictions.

1. Predict which set of scores had a higher mean.
   A. The scores on the multiple-choice form. B. The scores on the open-ended form.

2. Predict whether the difference you selected in question 1 is statistically significant at the .05 level or higher.
   A. Yes, the difference is statistically significant at the .05 level or higher.
   B. No, the difference is not statistically significant at the .05 level.

Data: The scores are given in Table 1. Although the exercise does not require you to consider who took which test first, you may be interested to know that the first ten subjects took the multiple-choice form first.

Table 1 *Number right scores of 20 students on two forms of the same test*

Student number	Scores on the multiple-choice form	Scores on the open-ended form
1	1	2
2	1	2
3	1	2
4	4	4
5	2	2
6	3	2
7	3	3
8	3	3
9	1	2
10	1	1
11	1	2
12	3	4
13	2	1
14	3	4
15	0	1
16	1	2
17	2	2
18	3	3
19	1	1
20	1	1

Calculations:

3. What is the mean of the scores on the multiple-choice form?

4. What is the mean of the scores on the open-ended form?

5. What is the observed value of *t*?

6. What is the critical value of *t* at the .05 level for a two-tailed test?

7. Is the difference statistically significant? If so, what is the highest level at which it is significant?

Checking Your Predictions:

8. Do your computations confirm your prediction in question 1?

9. Do your computations confirm your prediction in question 2?

Question for Discussion:

10. Do the results surprise you? Why? Why not?

Additional Analyses Required by Your Instructor: Your instructor may require you to perform additional analyses of the data in this exercise. If so, write the names of the statistics you are to compute and your answers in the spaces below.

11. Additional statistic to be computed:

    Answer:

12. Additional statistic to be computed:

    Answer:

Exercise 27 ONE-WAY ANALYSIS OF VARIANCE: TWO MEANS

Computer Experience and Computer Hassles[1]

Statistical Guide: To determine the significance of a set of differences among two or more means, we use analysis of variance (ANOVA). When ANOVA yields a probability of .05 or less, we usually reject the null hypothesis, which says that the difference(s) among the means were created by sampling (random) error.

In this exercise you will be using ANOVA to compare two means. This comparison also may be made with a *t* test, which was covered in earlier exercises. Although the values of *F* and *t* for a given comparison of two means will be different, they will both yield the same value of *p*.

Background Notes: Two samples of students attending a two-year technical college were obtained: (1) those who rated themselves as having "low experience" in using computers and (2) those who rated themselves as having "high experience." Students in both groups were administered the revised Computer Technology Hassles Scale, which is a list of 37 hassles some people have when using computers. The researchers were interested in whether the two groups differed in the number of hassles they have experienced.

Making Predictions: Before examining the data below, predict the results you will obtain. (When scientists make predictions, they are hypothesizing.) Note that your predictions are *not* right or wrong. Rather, they represent your best guess as to the outcomes you will obtain. After you perform the calculations, you will be able to determine whether the data support your predictions.

1. Predict whether there was a significant difference between the mean number of hassles reported by the high experience group and the mean number reported by the low experience group.
    A. Yes, there was a significant difference at the .05 level or higher.
    B. No, there was not a significant difference at the .05 level.

2. If you answered A to question 1, predict which group had the higher mean number of hassles.
    A. The high experience group.
    B. The low experience group.

Data: The numbers of hassles reported by students in each group are shown in Table 1.

---

[1]Data source: Dr. Collin T. Ballance, Nashville State Technical Institute, Nashville, TN. For more information on this topic, see Ballance, C. T., & Ballance, V. V. (1996). Psychology of computer use: XXXVII. Computer-related stress and amount of computer experience. *Psychological Reports, 78*, 969-970.

Table 1   *Number of computer technology hassles reported by students in two groups*

Number of hassles for "high experience" students	Number of hassles for "low experience" students
17	31
5	37
15	1
11	3
33	36
32	27
12	36
10	2
21	36
32	15
18	10
28	1
15	18
29	33
35	18
33	12
37	11
24	24
26	15
20	19
20	36
21	25
30	
15	
12	
36	
37	
17	
12	
25	
8	
36	
33	
37	
34	
31	

Calculations:

3. Before conducting an ANOVA, summarize the data by computing the means and standard deviations and writing them in Table 2.

   For the convenience of those who are using calculators instead of computers, the sum of scores and sum of squares for the high experience group are given below. You will need to compute the corresponding values for the low experience group before proceeding with the analysis.

   High experience group: $\Sigma X = 857$ and $\Sigma X^2 = 23,759$

Table 2 *Means and standard deviations for two groups*

Group	Mean	Standard Deviation
High experience		
Low experience		

4. Conduct a one-way ANOVA and enter the values to three decimal places in Table 3.

Table 3 *Analysis of variance table*

Source of variation	df	Sum of squares	Mean square	F	p
Between groups					
Within groups					
Total					

5. Is the difference between the means statistically significant (using a two-tailed test)? If yes, what is the highest probability level at which it is significant? (Remember that a lower probability represents a higher level of significance.)

6. Should the null hypothesis regarding difference between the means be rejected? If yes, what is the highest probability level at which it should be rejected?

Checking Your Predictions:

7. Do your computations confirm your prediction in question 1?

8. Do your computations confirm your prediction in question 2?

Question for Discussion:

9. Would you have found it easier to conduct a t test on the data in this exercise? Explain. (Remember that both analysis of variance and a t test will yield the same value of p when determining the significance of the difference between two means.)

Additional Analyses Required by Your Instructor: Your instructor may require you to perform additional analyses of the data in this exercise. If so, write the names the statistics you are to compute and your answers in the spaces below.

10. Additional statistic to be computed:

   Answer:

11. Additional statistic to be computed:

   Answer:

Exercise 28 ONE-WAY ANALYSIS OF VARIANCE: THREE MEANS

College Students' Seating Choices and Motivation to Achieve[1]

Statistical Guide: To determine the significance of a set of differences among two or more means, we use analysis of variance (ANOVA). When ANOVA yields a probability of .05 or less, we usually reject the null hypothesis, which says that the difference(s) among the means were created by sampling (random) error.[2]

Background Notes: The seating positions chosen by college freshmen in three sections of a required course were observed and recorded as either rows 1-2, rows 3-4, or rows 5-6. Students were administered a self-report questionnaire on their achievement motivation (that is, their desire to achieve). The possible range of scores was 0 (very low motivation) to 30 (very high motivation).

Making Predictions: Before examining the data below, predict the results you will obtain. (When scientists make predictions, they are hypothesizing.) Note that your predictions are *not* right or wrong. Rather, they represent your best guess as to the outcomes you will obtain. After you perform the calculations, you will be able to determine whether the data support your predictions.

1. Predict whether there was a significant difference in achievement motivation among the three groups of students (those who sat in rows 1-2 vs. those who sat in rows 3-4 vs. those who sat in rows 5-6).
   A. Yes, there was a significant difference at the .05 level or higher.
   B. No, there was not a significant difference at the .05 level.

2. If you answered A to question 1, predict which group had the highest mean achievement motivation scores.
   A. Those in rows 1-2.
   B. Those in rows 3-4.
   C. Those in rows 5-6.

---

[1]Data source: Dr. Charles I. Brooks, Department of Psychology, King's College, Wilkes-Barre, PA. For more information on this topic, see Burda, J. M., & Brooks, C. I. (1996). College classroom seating position and changes in achievement motivation over a semester. *Psychological Reports, 78,* 331-336.

[2]Various multiple comparisons tests are available for comparing the individual pairs of means for significance if ANOVA indicates overall significance.

Data: The achievement motivation scores are shown in Table 1.

Table 1 *Achievement motivation scores of three groups*

Scores of students in group A (Chose rows 1 or 2)	Scores of students in group B (Chose rows 3 or 4)	Scores of students in group C (Chose rows 5 or 6)
8	10	8
14	23	1
12	9	2
13	9	23
15	12	9
15	15	28
9	8	6
19	8	9
13	23	11
2	6	1
15	9	8
12	6	11
26	20	13
13	5	13
19	6	10
18	14	8
15	25	7
13	2	6
18	1	9
8	18	10
16	8	
1	11	
14	12	
19	6	
8	3	
8	15	
16		
8		
20		
11		
21		
24		
25		

Calculations:

3. Before conducting an ANOVA, summarize the data by computing the means and standard deviations and writing them in Table 2.

   For the convenience of those who are using calculators instead of computers, the sums of scores and sums of squares for groups A and B are given below. You will need to compute the corresponding values for group C before proceeding with the analysis.

   Group A: $\Sigma X_A = 468$ and $\Sigma X_A^2 = 7,744$
   Group B: $\Sigma X_B = 284$ and $\Sigma X_B^2 = 4,180$

Table 2 *Means and standard deviations for three groups*

Group	Mean	Standard Deviation
A (rows 1-2)		
B (rows 3-4)		
C (rows 5-6)		

4. Conduct a one-way ANOVA and enter the values to three decimal places in Table 3.

Table 3 *Analysis of variance table*

Source of variation	df	Sum of squares	Mean square	F	p
Between groups					
Within groups					
Total					

5. Is the set of differences statistically significant? If yes, what is the highest probability level at which it is significant?

6. Should the null hypothesis regarding the set of differences among the means be rejected? If yes, what is the highest probability level at which it should be rejected?

Checking Your Predictions:

7. Do your computations confirm your prediction in question 1?

8. Do your computations confirm your prediction in question 2?

Question for Discussion:

9. The one-way analysis of variance tests the set of all three differences overall. Would you be interested in comparing individual pairs of means such as group A vs. group B? Explain.

Additional Analyses Required by Your Instructor: Your instructor may require you to perform additional analyses of the data in this exercise. If so, write the names of the statistics you are to compute and your answers in the spaces below.

10. Additional statistic to be computed:

    Answer:

11. Additional statistic to be computed:

    Answer:

Exercise 29 SIGNIFICANCE OF THE DIFFERENCE BETWEEN VARIANCES

Attitudes of Teachers Toward Children with Disabilities[1]

Statistical Guide: By comparing the standard deviations for two groups, we can determine which group is more variable. (See Exercise 12 for more information on the standard deviation.) Just as two means may differ solely because of random sampling errors, so can two standard deviations. Thus, when two standard deviations are being compared, the null hypothesis says that the observed difference between two standard deviations is due to sampling error. We can test for the significance of the difference between two standard deviations using the test described below.

Background Notes: Samples of 54 music teachers and 56 physical education teachers responded to these statements: (1) "Children with emotional and behavioral disorders will benefit from the interaction with typical children" and (2) "I like having children with orthopedic handicaps in my classroom" on a four-point scale from 1 (strongly agree) to 4 (strongly disagree). For statement 1, the means for the music and physical education teachers were 2.7 and 2.2, respectively. For statement 2, the means for the music and physical education teachers were 2.0 and 2.4, respectively. Thus, on the average, the music teachers were more negative on the first statement, and the physical education teachers were more negative on the second statement.

Making Predictions: Before examining the data below, predict the results you will obtain. (When scientists make predictions, they are hypothesizing.) Note that your predictions are *not* right or wrong. Rather, they represent your best guess as to the outcomes you will obtain. After you perform the calculations, you will be able to determine whether the data support your predictions.

1. Predict which group was more variable in their responses to statement 1 given in the background notes above. (That is, in which group was the variation in opinions greater?)
   A. Music teachers.   B. Physical education teachers.

2. Predict whether the difference in variation in question 1 is statistically significant.
   A. Yes, it is statistically significant at the .05 level or higher.
   B. No, it is not statistically significant at the .05 level.

---

[1]Data source: Dr. Judy P. Chandler, Health and Physical Education, University of Kansas, Lawrence, KS. For more information on this topic, see Sideridis, G. D., & Chandler, J. P. (1996). Comparison of attitudes of teachers of physical and musical education toward inclusion of children with disabilities. *Psychological Reports, 78,* 768-770.

3. Predict which group was more variable in their responses to statement 2 given in the background notes above. (That is, in which group was the variation in opinions greater?)
A. Music teachers.   B. Physical education teachers.

4. Predict whether the difference variation in question 3 is statistically significant.
A. Yes, it is statistically significant at the .05 level or higher.
B. No, it is not statistically significant at the .05 level.

Data: The standard deviations are given in Table 1.

Table 1   *Standard deviations on two statements for two groups of teachers*

	SD for music teachers	*SD* for physical education teachers
1. Children with emotional and behavioral disorders will benefit from the interaction with typical children.	1.10	.95
2. I like having children with orthopedic handicaps in my classroom.	1.00	1.01

Calculations: To determine the significance of the difference between two standard deviations, we first compute the *variances* that correspond to each standard deviation. The variance is merely the square of each standard deviation. Then we compute F by dividing the larger variance by the smaller one (this is the *observed value* of F). We obtain the critical value of F using a table of critical values for analysis of variance, where df for each standard deviation is $n - 1$. Enter the table with the df for the larger variance as the *between-groups degrees of freedom*, and the df for the smaller variance as the *within-groups degrees of freedom*.[2] If the observed value of F is equal to or greater than the critical value, the difference is statistically significant.

5. What is the observed value of F for statement 1?

6. Is the value of F for the answer in question 5 statistically significant? If yes, what is the highest level at which it is significant?

7. What is the observed value of F for the statement 2?

8. Is the value of F for the answer in question 7 statistically significant? If yes, what is the highest level at which it is significant?

---

[2]As you can see, we are directly testing whether the difference between the *variances* is statistically significant. If it is, then the difference between the standard deviations is also significant.

Checking Your Predictions:

9. Do your computations confirm your prediction in question 1?

10. Do your computations confirm your prediction in question 2?

11. Do your computations confirm your prediction in question 3?

12. Do your computations confirm your prediction in question 4?

Question for Discussion:

13. Do the results surprise you? Why? Why not?

Additional Analyses Required by Your Instructor: Your instructor may require you to perform additional analyses of the data in this exercise. If so, write the names of the statistics you are to compute and your answers in the spaces below.

14. Additional statistic to be computed:

   Answer:

15. Additional statistic to be computed:

   Answer:

Exercise 30 STANDARD ERROR OF A PERCENTAGE AND 95% CONFIDENCE INTERVAL

Risk for Pregnancy Among Adolescents Who Had Been Sexually Abused[1]

Statistical Guide: The *standard error of a percentage* is a *margin of error* we use when interpreting percentages obtained by studying random samples. The formula for it is:

$$S_P = \sqrt{\frac{PQ}{n}}$$

Where: P is the percentage in question
Q is 100 minus P
n is the number of cases in the sample

If we multiply the standard error of a percentage by 1.96 and then add and subtract the product, we obtain an interval in which we can have 95% confidence that the true percentage lies.[2]

Here's an example:

In a survey, 54.2% of a sample of 120 voters approves of the way the president is handling foreign affairs. The standard error of the percentage is:

$$S_P = \sqrt{\frac{(54.2)(45.8)}{120}} = \sqrt{\frac{2482.36}{120}} = \sqrt{20.686} = 4.548 = 4.55$$

Multiplying this result by 1.96, we get 4.55 x 1.96 = 8.92.
Adding and subtracting from the percentage in question, we get:
54.2 + 8.92 = **63.12** and 54.2 – 8.92 = **45.28**.
Thus, we can have 95% confidence that the true percentage that approves is between 45.28% and 63.12%. This is called the *95% confidence interval* or *95% C.I.*

Background Notes: Two hundred 13- to 18-year-old sexually active females were the subjects in a study. Of them, 40 indicated that they had been sexually abused. Among other things, all subjects were asked if they were trying to conceive and if their boyfriend desired them to become pregnant.

Making Predictions: Before examining the data below, predict the results you will obtain. (When scientists make predictions, they are hypothesizing.) Note that your predictions are *not*

---

[1]Data source: Dr. David Y. Rainey, Forsyth Pediatrics and Adolescent Medicine, Winston-Salem, NC. For more information on this topic, see Rainey, D. Y., Stevens-Simon, C., & Kaplan, D. W. (1995). Are adolescents who report prior sexual abuse at higher risk for pregnancy? *Child Abuse and Neglect, 19*, 1283-1288.
[2]For a 99% confidence interval, use 2.58 as the multiplier.

right or wrong. Rather, they represent your best guess as to the outcomes you will obtain. After you perform the calculations, you will be able to determine whether the data support your predictions.

1. Predict which group had a higher percentage of females trying to conceive.
   A. Those who had been sexually abused.
   B. Those who had *not* been sexually abused.

2. Predict which group had a higher percentage of females with boyfriends who desired them to become pregnant.
   A. Those who had been sexually abused.
   B. Those who had *not* been sexually abused.

Data: The frequencies are shown in Tables 1 and 2.

Table 1 *Numbers of females trying to conceive*

	History of sexual abuse?	
	Yes ($n = 40$)	No ($n = 160$)
Number trying to conceive	14	18

Table 2 *Numbers of females with boyfriend desiring them to become pregnant*

	History of sexual abuse?	
	Yes ($n = 40$)	No ($n = 160$)
Number with boyfriend desiring her pregnancy	31	72

Calculations:

3. For each group, calculate the percentage of females who are trying to conceive and write the percentages in Table 3. Report your answers to one decimal place.

Table 3 *Percentages of females trying to conceive*

	History of sexual abuse?	
	Yes	No
Percentage trying to conceive		

4. For each group calculate the percentage of females who have boyfriends desiring them to become pregnant and write the percentages in Table 4. Report your answers to one decimal place.

Table 4 *Percentages of females with boyfriend desiring them to become pregnant*

	History of sexual abuse?	
	Yes	No
Percentage with boyfriend desiring her pregnancy		

5. Calculate the 95% confidence intervals for the percentages in Table 3 and enter them in Table 5.

Table 5 *95% confidence intervals for percentages in Table 3*

	History of sexual abuse?	
	Yes	No
Confidence intervals for percentages of females trying to conceive		

6. When the two confidence intervals do *not* overlap, we can have more confidence that the two groups are truly different than when they do overlap. Do the intervals in your answer to question 5 overlap?

7. Calculate the 95% confidence intervals for the percentages in Table 4 and enter them in Table 6.

Table 6 *95% confidence intervals for percentages in Table 4*

	History of sexual abuse?	
	Yes	No
Confidence intervals for percentages of females with a boyfriend desiring her pregnancy		

8. When the two confidence intervals do *not* overlap, we can have more confidence that the two groups are truly different than when they do overlap. Do the intervals in your answer to question 7 overlap?

Checking Your Predictions:

9. Do your computations confirm your prediction in question 1? Was your prediction supported by the overlapping or non-overlapping of the confidence intervals?

10. Do your computations confirm your prediction in question 2? Was your prediction supported by the overlapping or non-overlapping of the confidence intervals?

Question for Discussion:

11. Do the results surprise you? Why? Why not?

Additional Analyses Required by Your Instructor: Your instructor may require you to perform additional analyses of the data in this exercise. If so, write the names of the statistics you are to compute and your answers in the spaces below.

12. Additional statistic to be computed:

   Answer:

13. Additional statistic to be computed:

   Answer:

Exercise 31 ONE-WAY CHI SQUARE

Forms of Abuse Among Adolescent Females[1]

Statistical Guide: A one-way chi square (also known as a *goodness-of-fit chi square*) tests for the significance of the difference(s) among frequencies when subjects are classified in only one way. For example, we might ask a random sample of subjects for whom they plan to vote. If 60 say Candidate A and 30 say Candidate B, the *null hypothesis* asserts that the difference is due to the sampling errors. If a chi square test yields a *p* value of .05 or less, we usually reject the null hypothesis and declare the difference to be statistically significant. Note that in this example subjects are classified only according to whom they plan to vote for—they are classified in only one way. If we also classified them in terms of gender (i.e., how many men and how many women plan to vote for each candidate), we could conduct a two-way chi square, which is taken up in Exercise 32.

Background Notes: The subjects were 100 adolescent girls who presented themselves at an adolescent medical clinic at a large university health science center. They were from mixed racial and ethnic backgrounds and most were from lower socioeconomic groups. None was at the medical clinic to receive treatment for any form of abuse. They were administered a questionnaire that covered, among other things, abuse they had been subjected to.

Making Predictions: Before examining the data below, predict the results you will obtain. (When scientists make predictions, they are hypothesizing.) Note that your predictions are *not* right or wrong. Rather, they represent your best guess as to the outcomes you will obtain. After you perform the calculations, you will be able to determine whether the data support your predictions.

1. Predict which type of abuse was most frequently reported.
   A. Sexual. B. Verbal. C. Physical.

2. Predict whether the differences in the frequencies of girls reporting sexual, verbal, and physical abuse are statistically significant.
   A. Yes, they are significant at the .05 level or higher.
   B. No, they are not significant at the .05 level.

---

[1]Data source: Dr. Robert M. Cavanaugh, Jr., Department of Pediatrics, State University of New York, Syracuse, NY. For more information on this topic, see Cavanaugh, R. M., & Henneberger, P. K. (1996). Talking to teens about family problems. *Clinical Pediatrics*, February, 67-71.

Data: Forty-five of the 100 girls reported some type of abuse. The numbers of girls who reported each type of abuse (called the *observed frequencies*) are given in Table 1.

Table 1 *Observed types of abuse reported by 100 adolescent girls*

Sexual	Verbal	Physical
17	22	6

Calculations:

3. Calculate the expected frequencies and write them in Table 2.

Table 2 *Expected frequencies*

Sexual	Verbal	Physical

4. What is the observed value of chi square (that is, the value you calculated)?

5. What is the critical value of chi square at the .05 level (that is, the value you obtained from a table of critical values)?

6. Are the differences statistically significant at the .05 level or higher? If yes, what is the highest level at which they are significant?

7. Should the null hypothesis be rejected? If yes, what is the highest level at which it should be rejected?

Checking Your Predictions:

8. Do your computations confirm your prediction in question 1?

9. Do your computations confirm your prediction in question 2?

Question for Discussion:

10. Do the results surprise you? Why? Why not?

Additional Analyses Required by Your Instructor: Your instructor may require you to perform additional analyses of the data in this exercise. If so, write the names of the statistics you are to compute and your answers in the spaces below.

11. Additional statistic to be computed:

    Answer:

12. Additional statistic to be computed:

    Answer:

Exercise 32 CHI SQUARE TEST FOR A 2 BY 2 TABLE

Financial Concerns and Suicidal Thoughts of HIV+ Men[1]

Statistical Guide: Chi square is a test of the null hypothesis, which states that the observed differences resulted from sampling errors (i.e., random error). Chi square is used with nominal data (i.e., naming categories such as naming your state of residence, naming your religion, and so on). When the probability is .05 or less that the null hypothesis is correct, we reject it and declare the result to be statistically significant.

A two-way chi square in which we ask whether two populations are different on a dependent variable is sometimes called a *test of homogeneity*. It has this name because we are interested in whether the two samples are homogeneous on the dependent variable. A significant value of chi square indicates that they are probably *not* homogeneous. If we conclude they are *not* homogeneous, we are concluding that they are different from each other.

Background Notes: A sample of 44 asymptomatic (no symptoms) and 51 symptomatic HIV+ men completed a problem checklist. They checked off the problems they experienced during the previous month. The data below indicate how many in each group checked having financial problems and how many checked having suicidal thoughts.

Making Predictions: Before examining the data below, predict the results you will obtain. (When scientists make predictions, they are hypothesizing.) Note that your predictions are *not* right or wrong. Rather, they represent your best guess as to the outcomes you will obtain. After you perform the calculations, you will be able to determine whether the data support your predictions.

1. Predict whether you think the difference between the two groups on financial problems is statistically significant at the .05 level.
   A. Yes. B. No.

2. If yes to question 1, predict which group had a higher proportion that checked financial problems.
   A. Asymptomatic group. B. Symptomatic group.

---

[1]Data source: Kenneth I. Pakenham, Department of Psychology, The University of Queensland, Australia. For more information on this topic, see Pakenham, K. I., Dadds, M. R., & Terry, D. J. (1996). Adaptive demands along the HIV continuum. *Social Science and Medicine, 42*, 245-256.

3. Predict whether you think the difference between the two groups on suicidal thoughts is statistically significant at the .05 level.
   A. Yes. B. No.

4. If yes to question 3, predict which group had a higher proportion that checked suicidal thoughts.
   A. Asymptomatic group. B. Symptomatic group.

Data: The observed frequencies (numbers of cases) for financial problems are given in Table 1.

Table 1 *Numbers of men checking financial problems (observed frequencies)*

	Number who checked financial problems	Number who did *not* check financial problems
Asymptomatic ($n = 44$)	12	32
Symptomatic ($n = 51$)	23	28

The observed frequencies (numbers of cases) for suicidal thoughts are given in Table 2.

Table 2 *Numbers of men checking suicidal thoughts (observed frequencies)*

	Number who checked suicidal thoughts	Number who did *not* check suicidal thoughts
Asymptomatic ($n = 44$)	13	31
Symptomatic ($n = 51$)	14	37

Calculations:

5. Calculate the *expected frequencies* for the chi square test for *financial problems* and enter them in Table 3.

Table 3 *Expected frequencies for financial problems*

	Number who checked financial problems	Number who did *not* check financial problems
Asymptomatic ($n = 44$)		
Symptomatic ($n = 51$)		

6. What is the *observed value of chi square* for financial problems?

7. What is the *critical value of chi square* at the .05 level for financial problems?

8. For the data on financial problems, is chi square statistically significant at the .05 level?

9. Calculate the *expected frequencies* for the chi square test for *suicidal thoughts* and enter them in Table 4.

Table 4 *Expected frequencies for suicidal thoughts*

	Number who checked suicidal thoughts	Number who did *not* check suicidal thoughts
Asymptomatic ($n = 44$)		
Symptomatic ($n = 51$)		

10. What is the *observed value of chi square* for suicidal thoughts?

11. What is the *critical value of chi square* at the .05 level for suicidal thoughts?

12. For the data on suicidal thoughts, is chi square statistically significant at the .05 level?

Checking Your Predictions:

13. Based on the results of the chi square test, were your predictions in questions 1 and 2 confirmed? Explain.

14. Based on the results of the chi square test, were your predictions in questions 3 and 4 confirmed? Explain.

Question for Discussion:

15. In your opinion, would it be worthwhile to replicate this study with larger, more demographically diverse samples? Explain.

Additional Analyses Required by Your Instructor: Your instructor may require you to perform additional analyses of the data in this exercise. If so, write the names of the statistics you are to compute and your answers in the spaces below.

16. Additional statistic to be computed:

    Answer:

17. Additional statistic to be computed:

    Answer:

Exercise 33 CHI SQUARE TEST FOR A 2 BY 4 TABLE

Physicians' Willingness to Participate in Assisted Suicide and Their Religious Affiliations[1]

Statistical Guide: See Exercise 32 to review the chi square test of homogeneity.

Background Notes: A statewide survey of physicians on their willingness to participate in legalized physician-assisted suicide was conducted in Oregon where a law was passed permitting it under certain circumstances. (To date, the law has not been implemented because of legal challenges.) Among other things, the physicians in the survey were asked to name their religious affiliations. In this exercise, you will be analyzing the responses of the physicians in the four largest groups: Protestant, Jewish, Catholic, and none (no religious affiliation).

Making Predictions: Before examining the data below, predict the results you will obtain. (When scientists make predictions, they are hypothesizing.) Note that your predictions are *not* right or wrong. Rather, they represent your best guess as to the outcomes you will obtain. After you perform the calculations, you will be able to determine whether the data support your predictions.

1. Predict which group had the largest percentage willing to participate in legalized physician-assisted suicide.
   A. Protestant. B. Jewish. C. Catholic. D. None.

2. Predict which group had the smallest percentage willing to participate in legalized physician-assisted suicide.
   A. Protestant. B. Jewish. C. Catholic. D. None.

3. Predict whether the differences in willingness to participate across religious affiliation groups is statistically significant.
   A. Yes, it is statistically significant.
   B. No, it is not statistically significant.

---

[1]Data source: Dr. Melinda A. Lee, Center for Ethics in Health Care, University of Oregon, Portland, OR. For more information on this topic, see Lee, M. A., et al. (1996). Legalizing assisted suicide—Views of physicians in Oregon. *The New England Journal of Medicine, 334*, 310-315.

Data: The observed frequencies (numbers of cases) are shown in Table 1.

Table 1 *Numbers of physicians indicating willingness to participate classified according to religious affiliation (observed frequencies)*

	Might be willing to participate	Would *not* be willing to participate
Protestant ($n = 1,146$)	470	676
Jewish ($n = 198$)	132	66
Catholic ($n = 377$)	85	292
None ($n = 721$)	475	246

Calculations:

4. Before conducting a significance test, calculate the percentage of doctors in each religious group who might be willing to participate and enter them in Table 2. The percentage for Protestants has been calculated for you.

Table 2 *Percentages*

	Might be willing to participate
Protestant ($n = 1,146$)	41.0%
Jewish ($n = 198$)	
Catholic ($n = 377$)	
None ($n = 721$)	

5. Calculate the *expected frequencies* for the chi square test using the frequencies in Table 1 and enter them in Table 3.

Table 3 *Expected frequencies*

	Might be willing to participate	Would *not* be willing to participate
Protestant ($n = 1,146$)		
Jewish ($n = 198$)		
Catholic ($n = 377$)		
None ($n = 721$)		

6. What is the *observed value of chi square*?

7. What is the *critical value of chi square* at the .05 level?

8. Is chi square statistically significant at the .05 level?

9. Is chi square statistically significant at the .01 level?

10. Is chi square statistically significant at the .001 level?

Checking Your Predictions:

11. Did your analysis confirm your prediction in question 1?

12. Did your analysis confirm your prediction in question 2?

13. Did your analysis confirm your prediction in question 3?

Question for Discussion:

14. Did the results surprise you? Why? Why not?

Additional Analyses Required by Your Instructor: Your instructor may require you to perform additional analyses of the data in this exercise. If so, write the names of the statistics you are to compute and your answers in the spaces below.

15. Additional statistic to be computed:

   Answer:

16. Additional statistic to be computed:

   Answer:

Exercise 34 MEDIAN TEST

Favorite Colors and Depression[1]

Statistical Guide: The median test may be used to determine the statistical significance of the difference between two medians. To apply it, compute the median of *all scores* (for the two groups combined); this is known as the *grand median*. Then determine the number of individuals above the grand median and the number *not* above the grand median separately for each group. (If a person has a score that is equal to the median, count it as being "*not* above the median.") This yields four values, which can be recorded in a two-by-two table. Then conduct a two-way chi square test on the values. If *p* is .05 or less, we usually reject the null hypothesis, which says that the difference was created by random sampling error.

Background Notes: Two hundred and fifty-four undergraduates were surveyed. Of these, 12 indicated that yellow was their favorite color, and 12 indicated that black was their favorite color. All subjects also took the Beck Depression Inventory. Depression scores were interpreted as follows: 9 or less = no depression, 10 to 18 = mild/moderate depression, 19 to 29 = moderate/severe depression, and 30 or more = extremely severe depression. The researchers were interested in whether color choice was related to depression.

Making Predictions: Before examining the data below, predict the results you will obtain. (When scientists make predictions, they are hypothesizing.) Note that your predictions are *not* right or wrong. Rather, they represent your best guess as to the outcomes you will obtain. After you perform the calculations, you will be able to determine whether the data support your predictions.

1. Predict whether there was a significant difference between the median depression score of those who named yellow as their favorite color and the median of those who named black as their favorite color.
    A. Yes, there was a significant difference at the .05 level.
    B. No, there was not a significant difference at the .05 level.

2. If you answered yes to question 1, predict which group had the higher median.
    A. Those who named yellow as their favorite color.
    B. Those who named black as their favorite color.

---

[1]Data source: Dr. Rebecca F. Nolan, Department of Psychology, Louisiana State University, Shreveport, LA. For more information on this topic, see Nolan, R. F., Dai, Y., & Stanley, P. D. (1995). An investigation of the relationship between color choice and depression measured by the Beck Depression Inventory. *Perceptual and Motor Skills*, *81*, 1195-1200.

Data: The depression scores for the two groups are shown in Table 1.

Table 1 *Beck Depression Inventory scores for two groups*

Scores for those whose favorite color is yellow		Scores for those whose favorite color is black	
3	7	4	17
10	4	13	8
5	2	10	10
7	2	11	6
13	8	7	36
11	3	14	21

Calculations:

3. What is the grand median of all the scores in Table 1?

4. Enter in Table 2 the number of cases that are above the grand median and the number of cases that are not above the grand median for each group.

Table 2 *Numbers of cases above and not above the grand median*

	Number preferring yellow	Number preferring black
Number above the grand median		
Number *not* above the grand median		

5. What is the value of chi square for the data in Table 2?

6. Is chi square statistically significant? If yes, at what probability level?

Checking Your Predictions:

7. Do your computations confirm your prediction in question 1?

8. Do your computations confirm your prediction in question 2?

Questions for Discussion:

9. Do the results surprise you? Why? Why not?

10. What is the value of the means and medians for the two groups? Which is the better average for these data? Explain.

Additional Analyses Required by Your Instructor: Your instructor may require you to perform additional analyses of the data in this exercise. If so, write the names of the statistics you are to compute and your answers in the spaces below.

11. Additional statistic to be computed:

   Answer:

12. Additional statistic to be computed:

   Answer:

Exercise 35 MANN-WHITNEY *U* TEST

Racial Differences in Seeking Medical Assistance[1]

Statistical Guide: The Mann-Whitney *U* test determines whether the distribution of scores for one independent sample is significantly different from the distribution of another. When it yields a value of p that is .05 or less, we reject the null hypothesis.

Background Notes: Researchers who were investigating care-seeking for breast cancer symptoms measured *delay in seeking care* as the number of days between noticing a symptom and seeking medical care for it. The average subject was about 37 years old, and about two-thirds had completed high school or college. The data were recorded separately for African-American and White women.

Making Predictions: Before examining the data below, predict the results you will obtain. (When scientists make predictions, they are hypothesizing.) Note that your predictions are *not* right or wrong. Rather, they represent your best guess as to the outcomes you will obtain. After you perform the calculations, you will be able to determine whether the data support your predictions.

1. Do you think that there is a significant difference in *delay in seeking care* between African-American and White women?

2. If yes to question 1, which group do you think delayed longer?

---

[1]Data source: Dr. Diane Lauver, School of Nursing, University of Wisconsin, Madison, WI. For more information on this topic, see Lauver, D., & Youngran, T. (1995). Optimism and coping with a breast cancer symptom. *Nursing Research, 44*, 202-207. The data in this exercise are for a random sample of about 20% of the African-American and 20% of the White women studied. Complete data on these variables are included in Exercise 37.

Data: Table 1 shows the number of days between noticing a breast cancer symptom and seeking medical assistance for it.

Table 1 *Days of delay*

African-American ($n = 14$)	White ($n = 13$)
705	1116
315	154
206	42
186	33
50	32
35	21
23	14
14	9
11	8
7	3
3	1
2	0
1	0
0	

Calculations:

3. Note that because the distributions are skewed, the median is a better average than the mean. (For example, the mean number of days for African-American women is 111.3, which has been pulled up by a small number of women who delayed a very large number of days; thus, the mean is not a representative average). What is the median number of days for African-American women?

4. What is the median number of days for white women?

5. What is the smaller value of *U*?

6. Are the two distributions significantly different at the .05 level?

Checking Your Predictions:

7. Does your analysis confirm your prediction in question 1?

8. Does your analysis confirm your prediction in question 2?

Question for Discussion:

9. Do the results surprise you? Why? Why not?

Additional Analyses Required by Your Instructor: Your instructor may require you to perform additional analyses of the data in this exercise. If so, write the names of the statistics you are to compute and your answers in the spaces below.

10. Additional statistic to be computed:

    Answer:

11. Additional statistic to be computed:

    Answer:

Exercise 36 Comprehensive Analysis: I

Characteristics of Adolescent Male Gamblers[1]

Background Notes: More than 600 13-year-old boys attending schools throughout the Province of Quebec, Canada, were questioned about gambling. Thirty-three 13-year-old boys were identified as gamblers because they reported gambling once a week or more, having gambled $10 or more in one day, and having gambled often or very often with nonfamily members during the previous 12 months. A random sample of 35 13-year-old boys who did not meet these criteria was selected as a comparison group.

Other variables measured at age 13 using self-report questionnaires included: (1) *fighting,* (2) *alcohol and drug use,* (3) *vandalism,* and (4) *theft.* Teachers' and mothers' ratings of the boys at ages 10 and 11 were available on these variables: (5) *anxiety/withdrawal* and (6) *impulsivity.* For all variables, higher scores indicate a greater incidence or presence of the behaviors/traits. The researchers were interested in whether gamblers and non-gamblers differed on the six variables.[2] Data on socioeconomic status (SES) were also available.

Making Predictions: Before examining the data below, predict the results you will obtain. (When scientists make predictions, they are hypothesizing.) Note that your predictions are *not* right or wrong. Rather, they represent your best guess as to the outcomes you will obtain. After you perform the calculations, you will be able to determine whether the data support your predictions.

1. Do you think that the gamblers and non-gamblers differed significantly on *fighting*? If yes, which group do you think had the higher average score?

2. Do you think that the gamblers and non-gamblers differed significantly on *alcohol and drug use*? If yes, which group do you think had the higher average score?

3. Do you think that the gamblers and non-gamblers differed significantly on *vandalism*? If yes, which group do you think had the higher average score?

4. Do you think that the gamblers and non-gamblers differed significantly on *theft*? If yes, which group do you think had the higher average score?

---

[1]Data source: Dr. Frank Vitaro, School of Psycho-Education, University of Montreal, Montreal, Canada. For more information on this topic, see Vitaro, F., Ladouceur, R., & Bujold, A. (1996). Predictive and concurrent correlates of gambling in early adolescent boys. *Journal of Early Adolescence, 16,* 211-228.
[2]Additional variables were measured in the study.

5. Do you think that the gamblers and non-gamblers differed significantly on *anxiety/withdrawal*? If yes, which group do you think had the higher average score?

6. Do you think that the gamblers and non-gamblers differed significantly on *impulsivity*? If yes, which group do you think had the higher average score?

Data: The data are presented on the next two pages in Tables 2 and 3. For your information, Table 1 shows the *possible* range of scores.

Table 1 *Possible score values*

	Lowest possible score	Highest possible score
Fighting	6	24
Drugs/alcohol	3	12
Vandalism	6	24
Theft	10	40
Anxiety/withdrawal	0	10
Impulsivity	0	6
SES	18	102

Calculations: Your instructor will give you instructions on the statistics to compute.
WRITE THE INSTRUCTIONS HERE:

Table 2 *Raw scores for gamblers (n = 33)*

Subject	Fighting (Age 13)	Alcohol and Drug Use (Age 13)	Vandalism (Age 13)	Theft (Age 13)	Teacher Rating— Anxiety/ Withdrawal (Averages of ratings at ages 10 and 11)	Mother Rating— Anxiety/ Withdrawal (Averages of ratings at ages 10 and 11)	Teacher Rating— Impulsivity (Averages of ratings at ages 10 and 11)	Mother Rating— Impulsivity (Averages of ratings at ages 10 and 11)	SES
1	8	5	10	12	0	2.5	2	2	37
2	6	3	6	11	5	2.5	4	2	45
3	8	6	8	13	0.5	2.5	0	2.5	54
4	7	4	8	13	0.5	missing	2	missing	64
5	7	3	6	10	5	4	4.5	1.5	48
6	18	7	9	20	6.5	8	2	4.5	24
7	8	4	7	10	4	2	2.5	2	33
8	16	8	12	17	0.5	8	0.5	3	27
9	7	4	6	11	0	1	0.5	1.5	50
10	11	9	8	14	4.5	2.5	2	1	30
11	10	3	6	10	0	1	0	1	50
12	6	4	8	13	2.5	2	2.5	4	46
13	10	7	9	14	1.5	2.5	1.5	1.5	38
14	9	8	10	22	2.5	1.5	2	1.5	37
15	12	12	8	16	0	0.5	0	3	46
16	9	5	8	17	0.5	3	0.5	0	52
17	8	5	6	11	0	4.5	0	4	32
18	7	5	6	11	1	3.5	0	0	52
19	6	3	7	10	0.5	1	1	1	18
20	12	11	10	19	1	3	1.5	0.5	27
21	6	5	6	10	1	3	0.5	1.5	28
22	7	4	6	11	1.5	1	1.5	1	65
23	13	9	7	15	1	1.5	1	3.5	46
24	7	5	6	10	1.5	2	0	2.5	49
25	6	3	6	10	2	0	0	0	36
26	8	4	6	12	0	0	1.5	3	43
27	7	3	8	14	1.5	missing	1	missing	36
28	6	3	6	10	1	1.5	1	2	56
29	7	3	7	14	1	1.5	4	2	42
30	11	8	8	18	1.5	missing	2.5	missing	56
31	13	9	6	15	4.5	6	0	1	44
32	9	5	8	14	2.5	2.5	3.5	3.5	50
33	6	3	6	10	3	0	1	1	40

Table 3   *Raw scores for non-gamblers (n = 35)*

Subject	Fighting (Age 13)	Alcohol and Drug Use (Age 13)	Vandalism (Age 13)	Theft (Age 13)	Teacher Rating— Anxiety/ Withdrawal (Averages of ratings at ages 10 and 11)	Mother Rating— Anxiety/ Withdrawal (Averages of ratings at ages 10 and 11)	Teacher Rating— Impulsivity (Averages of ratings at ages 10 and 11)	Mother Rating— Impulsivity (Averages of ratings at ages 10 and 11)	SES
1	6	3	6	10	2	7	0	1	49
2	10	3	7	14	2.5	2	3.5	6	43
3	7	3	6	10	3	5	0	3	30
4	9	3	7	10	2	6	2.5	4	43
5	6	3	6	10	6	7	3.5	6	51
6	7	3	6	12	7	missing	2.5	missing	41
7	6	3	6	10	3	6	6	4	27
8	7	4	7	11	8	8	3.5	4	41
9	6	4	6	10	0	2.5	1	2.5	45
10	6	3	7	10	2.5	2	0	0	49
11	6	4	6	11	0	0.5	1	2.5	62
12	6	3	6	10	3.5	2	0	1	74
13	8	3	6	10	7	4	2	3.5	43
14	6	3	6	11	1.5	3	2.5	1.5	60
15	7	3	6	11	0	2	2.5	1.5	52
16	6	7	7	15	1	3	0.5	1	40
17	6	6	6	13	1.5	2	1	3	29
18	6	8	7	13	1	missing	1.5	missing	50
19	6	3	6	10	0	1.5	0	0.5	50
20	6	3	6	10	4.5	3	2	2	34
21	6	4	6	10	2	3	0	0	59
22	8	3	6	10	3.5	2.5	2	0.5	41
23	6	6	6	13	3.5	5.5	1	1.5	56
24	6	7	6	12	7	2.5	3	0.5	40
25	6	3	6	10	0.5	4	0.5	3	60
26	6	3	8	10	4	5	2	2.5	47
27	8	4	6	11	6.5	1	2	1.5	33
28	9	5	6	10	0	2	2	1	31
29	7	3	6	10	2.5	6	2	3	43
30	6	3	6	10	1.5	7	0.5	2.5	50
31	7	3	6	10	1	2	0	1	61
32	13	7	9	17	3	7.5	0.5	3.5	41
33	8	4	7	10	4	7	0.5	0.5	50
34	6	3	6	10	4.5	5	4	2.5	20
35	6	4	7	10	1.5	2.5	0	1	57

Checking Your Predictions:

7. Based on your answers, was your prediction in question 1 confirmed? Explain.

8. Based on your answers, was your prediction in question 2 confirmed? Explain.

9. Based on your answers, was your prediction in question 3 confirmed? Explain.

10. Based on your answers, was your prediction in question 4 confirmed? Explain.

11. Based on your answers, was your prediction in question 5 confirmed? Explain.

12. Based on your answers, was your prediction in question 6 confirmed? Explain.

Questions for Discussion:

13. Do the results of this study surprise you? Explain.

14. What are the possible implications of this study?

Exercise 37   Comprehensive Analysis: II

Care-Seeking for
Breast Cancer Symptoms[1]

Background Notes: Researchers who were interested in the relationship between optimism and care-seeking behavior studied 135 women at a breast surgery clinic in an urban hospital. The researchers measured a number of variables including:

1. *Delay in seeking care.* Measured as the number of days between noticing a symptom and seeking medical assistance.
2. *Optimism.* Measured with the Life Orientation Test (LOT). Sample item: "In uncertain times, I usually expect the best." Each of the eight items was scored on a five-point scale from 0 (strongly disagree) to 4 (strongly agree). Then, for each woman, the scores on the eight items were averaged, yielding scores from 0 to 4.
3. *Age.* Measured in years.
4. *Race.* Coded as W = White, A = African-American.
5. *Education.* Coded from 0 (less than 8th grade) through 7 (doctorate or professional degree). Note that 3 = high school diploma.

Making Predictions: Before examining the data below, predict the results you will obtain. (When scientists make predictions, they are hypothesizing.) Note that your predictions are *not* right or wrong. Rather, they represent your best guess as to the outcomes you will obtain. After you perform the calculations, you will be able to determine whether the data support your predictions.

1. Predict the relationship between optimism and delay.
   A. A direct relationship (those who were more optimistic delayed more, and those who were less optimistic delayed less).
   B. An inverse relationship (those who were more optimistic delayed less, and those who were less optimistic delayed more).
   C. There is no relationship.

2. Predict the relationship between age and delay.
   A. A direct relationship (those who were older delayed more, and those who were younger delayed less).
   B. An inverse relationship (those who were older delayed less, and those who were younger delayed more).
   C. There is no relationship.

---

[1]Data source: Dr. Diane Lauver, School of Nursing, University of Wisconsin, Madison, WI. For more information on this topic, see Lauver, D., & Youngran, T. (1995). Optimism and coping with a breast cancer symptom. *Nursing Research, 44,* 202-207.

3. Predict the relationship between education and delay.
   A. A direct relationship (those who had more education delayed more and those who had less education delayed less).
   B. An inverse relationship (those who had more education delayed less and those who had less education delayed more).
   C. There is no relationship.

4. Make a prediction about the relationship between delay and race.

Data: The data are presented on the following five pages. Your instructor will either ask you to ignore the column labeled "Transformed Delay" or give you an explanation of it, depending on your course objectives.

Calculations: Your instructor will give you instructions on the statistics to compute.
WRITE THE INSTRUCTIONS HERE:

Subject Number	Delay (# of days)	Trans-formed Delay	Optimism (LOT score)	Age (years)	Race (White = 0, Black = 1)	Education (0 to 7)
1	15	2.8	2.8	28	0	3
2	353	5.9	2.5	29	1	4
3	3	1.4	3.0	40	0	2
4	0	0.0	3.9	54	0	6
5	154	5.0	1.9	62	0	2
6	0	0.0	3.1	50	0	2
7	105	4.7	2.5	38	1	3
8	10	2.4	2.5	65	1	2
9	292	5.7	1.8	49	1	4
10	28	3.4	2.5	30	0	2
11	21	3.1	2.4	19	1	3
12	5	1.8	2.1	43	1	2
13	12	2.6	4.0	40	0	5
14	15	2.8	2.6	76	1	1
15	4	1.6	2.6	56	1	3
16	1	0.7	2.2	32	1	3
17	242	5.5	1.8	56	0	2
18	1	0.7	2.2	38	0	3
19	50	3.9	3.8	53	1	3
20	78	4.4	1.9	61	1	2
21	50	3.9	2.1	29	1	3
22	1	0.7	3.8	39	1	2
23	2,538	7.8	2.1	27	1	3
24	5	1.8	3.8	53	0	4
25	3	1.4	2.0	36	1	4
26	113	4.7	2.2	38	1	2
27	0	0.0	1.8	29	1	3
28	4	1.6	2.1	43	0	5
29	90	4.5	3.5	61	0	3
30	7	2.1	2.8	43	0	3

Continued on next page.

Subject Number	Delay (# of days)	Trans- formed Delay	Optimism (LOT score)	Age (years)	Race (White = 0, Black = 1)	Education (0 to 7)
31	1	0.7	3.4	40	0	6
32	184	5.2	3.8	30	0	4
33	705	6.6	1.6	46	1	4
34	186	5.2	2.6	21	1	3
35	0	0.0	1.9	43	1	2
36	0	0.0	0.6	31	1	5
37	130	4.9	3.2	52	1	2
38	128	4.9	1.5	33	0	3
39	264	5.6	3.5	26	1	5
40	547	6.3	1.6	50	1	1
41	0	0.0	3.8	43	0	4
42	212	5.4	2.6	32	1	2
43	4	1.6	2.5	41	1	3
44	260	5.6	2.1	28	1	4
45	57	4.1	3.9	57	0	4
46	7	2.1	2.9	29	1	4
47	25	3.9	2.4	69	1	1
48	6	2.0	1.9	32	1	3
49	70	4.3	1.8	52	0	3
50	2	1.1	2.6	25	1	2
51	153	5.0	3.0	33	0	5
52	51	4.0	2.5	19	1	4
53	11	2.5	2.2	19	1	4
54	0	0.0	1.2	37	0	4
55	15	2.8	2.2	26	1	5
56	2	1.1	2.9	21	0	3
57	14	2.7	2.9	24	1	3
58	138	4.9	2.0	42	0	4
59	50	3.9	3.5	42	0	5
60	1,116	7.0	1.6	28	0	3

Continued on next page.

Subject Number	Delay (# of days)	Trans- formed Delay	Optimism (LOT score)	Age (years)	Race (White = 0, Black = 1)	Education (0 to 7)
61	7	2.1	1.4	31	1	3
62	56	4.0	3.0	29	0	3
63	183	5.2	1.5	59	1	2
64	21	3.1	1.0	22	0	3
65	9	2.3	2.5	25	0	6
66	11	2.5	2.4	36	0	2
67	1	0.7	3.1	20	1	3
68	1	0.7	2.5	35	0	3
69	14	2.7	2.2	33	1	2
70	5	1.8	2.8	31	0	4
71	27	3.3	3.5	41	0	3
72	3	1.4	2.0	30	0	2
73	35	3.6	2.2	70	0	3
74	2	1.1	1.5	37	1	3
75	196	5.3	2.2	33	0	3
76	17	2.9	2.4	34	1	4
77	36	3.6	1.6	32	1	2
78	5	1.8	2.0	27	1	2
79	8	2.2	2.8	35	1	3
80	0	0.0	3.0	22	0	4
81	1	0.7	2.9	36	0	3
82	1	0.7	3.2	46	0	3
83	2	1.1	2.2	24	0	5
84	4	1.6	3.0	24	0	5
85	3	1.4	3.1	33	0	5
86	105	4.7	2.9	52	0	6
87	16	2.8	1.2	20	1	2
88	1	0.7	2.9	41	0	5
89	23	3.2	2.1	23	1	2
90	1	0.7	1.5	26	0	3

Continued on next page.

Subject Number	Delay (# of days)	Trans-formed Delay	Optimism (LOT score)	Age (years)	Race (White = 0, Black = 1)	Education (0 to 7)
91	2	1.1	2.8	24	1	2
92	11	2.5	2.8	37	1	4
93	32	3.5	3.5	32	0	7
94	30	3.4	2.8	48	0	4
95	0	0.0	2.5	38	0	3
96	33	3.5	1.5	42	1	1
97	0	0.0	1.9	35	1	1
98	50	3.9	3.0	38	1	3
99	244	5.5	3.4	22	1	4
100	1	0.7	3.6	44	0	6
101	8	2.2	2.6	36	0	4
102	950	6.9	2.2	36	0	2
103	114	4.7	1.5	28	0	4
104	141	5.0	3.6	32	0	5
105	1	0.7	2.2	24	0	2
106	197	5.3	2.1	40	1	2
107	0	0.0	3.6	51	1	1
108	179	5.2	2.1	24	1	2
109	199	5.3	1.0	27	1	3
110	53	4.0	4.0	60	1	2
111	88	4.5	2.6	38	0	6
112	14	2.7	3.9	31	0	4
113	29	3.4	2.4	53	1	1
114	42	3.8	2.6	23	0	3
115	315	5.8	1.4	30	1	1
116	85	4.5	2.0	28	1	2
117	20	3.0	2.2	41	1	4
118	40	3.7	1.8	28	0	2
119	15	2.8	2.2	40	1	2
120	14	2.7	3.5	51	1	5

Continued on next page.

Subject Number	Delay (# of days)	Trans-formed Delay	Optimism (LOT score)	Age (years)	Race (White = 0 Black = 1)	Education (0 to 7)
121	2	1.1	3.5	43	1	4
122	31	3.5	3.0	28	0	3
123	4	1.6	2.6	31	1	3
124	1	0.7	2.9	45	1	6
125	9	2.3	3.5	29	1	2
126	0	0.0	3.2	42	1	4
127	2	1.1	3.1	46	0	3
128	7	2.1	2.6	32	0	4
129	21	3.1	2.9	48	0	2
130	141	5.0	2.0	72	0	1
131	3	1.4	2.0	23	1	1
132	206	5.3	2.5	29	1	3
133	5	1.8	3.0	43	0	4
134	43	3.8	3.2	25	1	1
135	11	2.5	2.5	29	0	4

Checking Your Predictions:

5. Based on your analysis, was your prediction in question 1 confirmed? Explain.

6. Based on your analysis, was your prediction in question 2 confirmed? Explain.

7. Based on your analysis, was your prediction in question 3 confirmed? Explain.

8. Based on your analysis, was your prediction in question 4 confirmed? Explain.

Questions for Discussion:

9. Do the results of this study surprise you? Explain.

10. What are the possible implications of this study?

Exercise 38   Comprehensive Analysis: III

Attitudes Toward Math, Math Achievement, and Expected Grades[1]

Background Notes: Fifty-six college students who were enrolled in a large state university took a pretest in their introductory statistics class. The students had a variety of majors such as social work, nursing, criminal justice, education, and counseling. The majority were undergraduates and more than 80% were female. The pretest consisted of 14 items such as:

1. We obtain a *product* when we perform which mathematical operation?
   A. addition B. subtraction C. multiplication D. division E. not given
2. –9/3 equals
   A. 3 B. 6 C. –3 D. –6 E. not given
3. If $150 - X = 101$, what does X stand for?
   A. 251 B. 151 C. 49 D. 149 E. not given

Each student answered all 14 items twice—once in multiple-choice form and once in open-ended form (without choices). A random half took the multiple-choice form first while the rest took the open-ended form first.

To measure attitudes toward math, students also answered these two questions:

Which choice best describes your attitude toward math?
A. very positive B. somewhat positive C. neutral D. somewhat negative E. very negative

How did you feel when you first learned that statistics was a required class in your major field of study?
A. very positive B. somewhat positive C. neutral D. somewhat negative E. very negative

Finally, expected grade was measured with this question:
What grade do you expect to earn in this class? (Circle one.)
A+ A A– B+ B B– C+ C C– D+ D D– F

Making Predictions: Before examining the data below, predict the results you will obtain. (When scientists make predictions, they are hypothesizing.) Note that your predictions are *not* right or wrong. Rather, they represent your best guess as to the outcomes you will obtain. After you perform the calculations, you will be able to determine whether the data support your predictions.

1. Predict whether scores on the test are related to attitudes toward math.
   A. Yes, they are related.
   B. No, they are not related.

---

[1]Data source: Dr. Fred Pyrczak, Division of Educational Foundations and Interdivisional Studies, California State University, Los Angeles. Note that a random sample of the data in this exercise was presented in Exercise 26.

2. Predict whether scores on the test are related to expected grades.
   A. Yes, they are related.
   B. No, they are not related.

3. Do you think that taking the multiple-choice items first had an effect on the open-ended test scores? If yes, did it make the open-ended test easier?

Data: The data are presented here. Note that in column 2, "Form Taken First," M = multiple-choice form and OE = open-ended form.

Student Number	Form Taken First	Open-Ended Test Score	Multiple-Choice Test Score	Attitude Toward Math	Attitude Toward Taking Statistics	Expected Grade
1	M	10	9	B	D	A
2	M	10	10	missing	missing	A+
3	M	11	11	B	C	A
4	M	12	11	A	B	A
5	M	9	9	D	D	B+
6	OE	10	9	B	C	A
7	OE	12	10	A	B	A
8	OE	7	8	A	B	A
9	OE	12	10	A	A	A+
10	OE	10	8	A	C	A
11	OE	10	9	C	C	A
12	OE	8	10	C	D	B
13	OE	12	12	B	C	A+
14	OE	6	5	D	C	A
15	OE	10	10	D	D	A+
16	M	11	12	D	D	B+
17	M	11	11	B	C	A+
18	M	10	10	B	B	B
19	M	11	10	A	C	A
20	M	7	7	D	D	A−

Continued on next page.

131

Student Number	Form Taken First	Open-Ended Test Score	Multiple-Choice Test Score	Attitude Toward Math	Attitude Toward Taking Statistics	Expected Grade
21	M	11	10	B	B	A
22	M	8	7	A	A	A+
23	M	8	9	D	C	A
24	M	13	13	A	B	A
25	M	9	9	C	C	A−
26	M	10	8	D	E	A
27	M	9	8	C	C	A
28	M	13	11	C	D	A
29	M	8	7	D	D	A+
30	OE	11	12	A	A	A+
31	OE	12	11	D	C	B
32	OE	12	12	B	D	B+
33	OE	13	13	A	A	A+
34	OE	12	13	B	B	A
35	OE	13	12	B	C	B
36	OE	11	10	B	D	A
37	OE	9	7	B	B	A
38	OE	11	9	A	A	A
39	OE	12	11	D	E	B
40	M	11	12	D	D	A
41	M	10	9	D	C	A+
42	M	12	11	B	B	A−
43	M	12	12	A	C	A
44	M	13	13	E	E	B
45	M	9	10	D	C	B+
46	M	13	12	C	D	B+
47	M	10	8	A	A	A
48	M	9	8	E	E	A+
49	OE	11	12	E	E	B+

Continued on next page.

Exercise 38   Comprehensive Analysis: III

Student Number	Form Taken First	Open-Ended Test Score	Multiple-Choice Test Score	Attitude Toward Math	Attitude Toward Taking Statistics	Expected Grade
50	OE	9	8	C	C	A
51	OE	9	9	C	D	B+
52	OE	11	11	C	C	A+
53	OE	12	12	B	B	A
54	OE	12	12	B	C	B
55	OE	9	8	C	C	A
56	OE	11	10	E	E	B

Calculations: Your instructor will give you instructions on the statistics to compute.
WRITE THE INSTRUCTIONS HERE:

Checking Your Predictions:

4. Based on your analysis, was your prediction in question 1 confirmed? Explain.

5. Based on your analysis, was your prediction in question 2 confirmed? Explain.

6. Based on your analysis, was your prediction in question 3 confirmed? Explain.

Questions for Discussion:

7. Do the results of this study surprise you? Explain.

8. What are the possible implications of this study?

NOTES

NOTES

NOTES

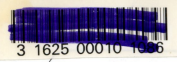
Other books of interest from Pyrczak Publishing

Success at Statistics
A Worktext with Humor

Making Sense of Statistics
A Conceptual Overview

Interpreting Basic Statistics
A Guide and Workbook Based on Excerpts from Journal Articles

Statistics with a Sense of Humor
A Humorous Workbook and Guide to Study Skills

Understanding Research Methods
An Overview of the Essentials

Educational and Psychological Research
A Cross Section of Journal Articles for Analysis and Evaluation

Social Science Research
A Cross Section of Journal Articles for Discussion and Evaluation

Writing Business Research Reports
A Guide to Scientific Writing

Interpreting Social and Behavioral Research
A Guide and Workbook Based on Excerpts from Journal Articles

Writing Empirical Research Reports
A Basic Guide for Students of the Social and Behavioral Sciences

For a descriptive brochure on any of the above, please write to
Pyrczak Publishing, P.O. Box 39731, Los Angeles, CA 90039